To The B. H. Carroll Theologue
Institute
with best wishes for the many
students you will help see
that the church is supposed
to be fun.

Brett Younger

Who Moved My Pulpit?

Smyth & Helwys Publishing, Inc.
6316 Peake Road
Macon, Georgia 31210-3960
1-800-747-3016
©2004 by Smyth & Helwys Publishing
All rights reserved.
Printed in the United States of America.

The paper used in this publication meets the minimum requirements of
American National Standard for Information Sciences—
Permanence of Paper for Printed Library Materials.
ANSI Z39.48–1984. (alk. paper)

Library of Congress Cataloging-in-Publication Data

Younger, Brett, 1961-
Who moved my pulpit? : a hilarious look at
ministerial life / by Brett Younger.
p. cm.
ISBN 1-57312-428-1 (pbk. : alk. paper)
1. Pastoral theology—Baptists—Humor.
I. Title.
BV4015.Y66 2004
252'.2'0207—dc22

2004001349

Who Moved My Pulpit?

A Hilarious Look at Ministerial Life

Brett Younger

SMYTH&HELWYS
PUBLISHING, INCORPORATED   MACON, GEORGIA

To Carol,

because the other book I dedicated to you

was never published

(contents)

A Funny Thing Happened on the Way to the Pulpit

It's nine o'clock on Tuesday morning. The setting is the First Baptist Church of the biggest city in a state where Baptist churches out-number gas stations. A worship-planning meeting is about to begin. Staff members gather around a long oak table. The minister of administration wears a brown three-piece suit. He has a cup of coffee—black, no sugar. The minister of youth is in cut-off shorts and a Hard Rock Cafe T-shirt. She has an iced caramel macchiato espresso. The two of them don't sit together.

The meeting always begins with the pastor reading the text for the next Sunday's service. This week's reading is from 2 Samuel 6. When he gets to the part about David dancing girded with a linen ephod, the minister of children giggles. The pastor explains that the focus of Sunday's worship service will be "God's kind of joy."

Then he eases into an idea he knows some of them won't like: "I know we don't usually do this, but since the service is about joy, I'd like for us to actually welcome one another during the welcome time."

"We are losing our sense of reverence," warns the minister of administration.

Ignoring him, the minister of senior adults suggests that they greet one another as they did in the early church: "The Lord be with you"; "and also with you."

The minister of preschoolers has a different idea: "Let's say 'God loves you and I do, too' and then hug."

The look on the minister of administration's face makes it clear that he's not in favor of hugging under any circumstances. The pastor drops the idea of welcoming one another.

They agree that there ought to be a lot of music in a service about joy, but they disagree over the opening hymn. The minister of senior adults wants "Joyful, Joyful, We Adore Thee." The minister of youth makes a case for "Lord of the Dance." The discussion heats up until the pastor, who often referees, says, "We'll sing them both."

The staff discusses several Scripture readings. The minister of children wants Psalm 2:4, "God who sits in heaven laughs." The idea of God laughing strikes the minister of administration and the minister to the extremely wealthy as sacrilegious. Then the minister of special ministries reads Psalm 149, which doesn't include laughing but mentions dancing in worship.

For the Gospel reading, the minister of the middle-aged wants John 15: "I have said these things to you so that my joy may be in you, and that your joy may be complete." It would do, but the minister of youth finds the passage on which they all agree—Luke 7, in which Jesus complains that he played the flute and they wouldn't dance.

The children's minister says she is open to suggestions for the children's time. The minister of administration complains, as he does each week, that a children's sermon is inappropriate in formal worship. "It is uncouth and unrefined," he says with a frown.

Everyone ignores the minister of administration. The associate minister of youth says that in keeping with the dancing imagery in the text, he would be willing to perform a speech from the movie *Footloose*, which he has seen twelve times. Without prompting, he begins: "Dancing is a celebration . . . of just about everything. Aren't we told in Psalm 149, 'Praise God's name with dancing'? And there was King David in the book of Samuel . . . leaping and dancing before God. In Ecclesiastes we're told, 'There is a time to dance.' That's the way it was in the beginning, the way it's always been, and the way it should be, now and forever." The associate minister of youth looks like Kevin Bacon, so it's with regret that the staff passes on the children's time from *Footloose*.

The pastor asks that quotations be printed in the order of worship to direct the worshipers' attention to joy. The minister of education, who considers himself an expert in pithy quotes and whose suggestions are rejected each week, says, "I have three profound, insightful quotes: Will Rogers—'We're only here for a spell, get all the good laughs you can'; H. L. Mencken—'Puritanism is the impulse to punish those who have a superior capacity for happiness'; and Mark Twain—'The good life is good friends, good books, and a sleepy conscience.'"

The pastor isn't sure that Rogers, Mencken, or Twain capture where he hopes to go. Fortunately, the minister of the arts offers a quotation from Methchild of Magdeburg: "I cannot dance, O Lord, unless you lead me. If you wish me to leap joyfully, let me see you dance and sing."

The service looks good. It has a clear focus, but there's also movement and variety. They need something more, but what they need can't be typed into an order of worship.

On Sunday morning, the pastor of the First Baptist Church stands to preach. The service has gone well. When they sang "Joyful, Joyful," the associate youth minister, who thought it high church, didn't look joyful. When they sang "Lord of the Dance," the minister of administration, who thought the song low church, grimaced.

Now the pastor reads the Scripture and begins a sermon that he knows is overly dependent on Frederick Buechner, but it's too late to worry about it now:

Israel adored David like no other king Israel ever had. The story of how he captured Jerusalem helps us understand why. Jerusalem was a major plum for the young king—a town in the hills considered so untakable that the people of Jerusalem had a saying to the effect that a blind man and a crippled man could hold it against the US Marines. Just to remind people who had finally taken it, David's first move was to, with all humility, change its name to "The City of David."

David's second move was a brilliant maneuver, giving his victory the stamp of God's approval. He brought out the ark. Anyone who's seen *Raiders of the Lost Ark* knows that no one knows what was in it, but it was as close as Israel ever got to an official symbol of God's presence. David had the ark loaded onto a custom-built cart and made a parade of it, complete with horns, harps, and cymbals, not to mention himself high-stepping out in front. Buechner says David looked "like the Mayor of Dublin on Saint Patrick's Day." When they came into town, they found that David had set up a big tent with refreshments. Just so nobody would forget who was picking up the tab, he did most of the praying himself.

So far it was nothing a good public relations director couldn't have dreamed up, but the next thing was something else. David stripped down to his skivvies, and with everybody looking on, he danced. Maybe it started out as just another public relations ploy, but not for long.

With trumpets blaring and drums beating, it was Camelot all over again. For once David didn't have to drag God in for politics' sake, because it was obvious that this time God was already there. How they cut loose together, David and God, whirling around before the ark in such utter abandon that they almost caught fire. The service wasn't turning out exactly like David had planned. Something was happening that wasn't in the order of worship.

At this point, the pastor's mind starts to wander. His thoughts often meander during sermons, but not nearly as much as those of his listeners and never too far from the text. He thinks of David in the middle of a worship service dancing in his underwear. Then he wonders, "What would happen if I stripped down to my boxers and danced a jig?" Would he do a disco step or a pirouette or two? Could he remember how to do the Macarena?

Then he realizes that the dance itself would not be the primary issue. Being in his underwear would be the attention grabber. Would people go running out of the sanctuary, or would they finally move to the front rows? He could imagine Mrs. Lyles beckoning the head usher, "Would you please call the police?"

What would the deacons think? Would the minister of administration faint? Would mothers cover their daughters' eyes? Would the minister of counseling rush to the front to talk to him about his stress level?

Then he catches the eye of his wife seated on the second row. Whatever Michal said to David was nothing compared to what his beloved wife would say. Would she call her parents? No, she would call his parents. What would his children think? They had seen him dance in his boxers, but it had been a while.

Then, for reasons that he was never able to explain, he realizes that he is wearing the boxer shorts his wife gave him on Valentine's Day—the ones with the big red hearts. That's when he starts laughing.

Have you ever gotten tickled at the worst possible time? This is Mary Tyler Moore at the funeral of Chuckles the Clown. Maybe you've gotten the giggles during a wedding and the harder you try to stop, the more you laugh. The pastor is shaking with laughter that starts at the bottom of his feet and takes over his whole body.

He realizes he's in trouble. The minister of administration is not smiling. The preacher tries to explain that he is laughing because he just imagined how they would react if he danced like David did. A few members of the congregation chuckle nervously, but not many. He tries to regain his composure but then pictures himself dancing and starts laughing again.

He isn't going to be able to get back to the sermon. He wishes that he had listened to the scene from *Footloose*. He needs something to wrap it up. He remembers a quote from Martin Luther.

Still giggling, he says, "Martin Luther argued, 'If you're not allowed to laugh in heaven, I don't want to go there.'"

Judging from their reactions, most of the people at First Baptist Church don't share Luther's opinion. They aren't laughing.

When the service is finally, mercifully over, most of the people go out the side door so they won't have to speak to the pastor. When he gets into the car to drive home, he expects his wife to give him the dressing down that Michal gave David—"You really did yourself proud this time, laughing boy"—but instead, she starts laughing. She tries to make sense of it all. "We try so hard to keep everything under control that we miss the fun of it. We plan. We program. We work. We don't dance enough. We don't laugh enough. The foolish, laughing, dancing, holy moments are a taste of the goodness of God."

(introduction)

This Isn't What I Signed Up For

Before next Sunday, you're supposed to:

• write a piece for the website that no one will read.
• counsel a couple who shouldn't get married but who have already bought the dress.
• explain to the deacons that the preschool rooms can't go another year without new carpeting.
• explain to the communion guild that they can go another year without gold-plated serving trays.
• meet with the Habitat for Humanity ministers' committee (would you live in a house built by pastors?).
• visit someone who is having knee replacement surgery (should ministers show up for operations on appendages?).
• prepare a Bible study on Habakkuk (which you keep misspelling).
• create an excuse to miss an associational meeting.
• prepare to tell the story of the Ethiopian eunuch to the four-year-old Sunday school class (who picks these texts?).

During your free time, you are to prepare a sermon. You know that you should:

- exegete the text.
- parse the Greek.
- examine textual variants.
- study the historical setting.
- review questions of date and authorship.
- check the commentaries (what does Walter Brueggemann think?).
- imagine your way back into the story.
- organize your thoughts (what does William Willimon think?).
- outline.
- select a key idea before you even begin writing.

Some weeks, though, you don't get to every step (what does desperatepreacher.com think?).

If you have extra time, you hope to:

- make an appearance at Seniors' Game Day, because you've been told you "must play a hand or two of forty-two."
- drop in on the Monday meditation group to see if they are as "transcendental" as you have been told.
- drive for the youth scavenger hunt (so a seventeen-year-old will not drive at the youth scavenger hunt).
- visit two shut-in members of the church who think you should have visited by now.
- read Max Lucado's latest book (which has been sitting on your desk for several months), a Henri Nouwen classic, or at least Martin Marty's column at the back of *Christian Century*.

While you end up doing nothing on your "hope to do" list, you will have the joyful privilege of:

- debriefing Sunday's service at length with a self-appointed lay worship consultant.

- explaining to the secretary again that if a caller mispronounces your name it is probably a salesperson to whom you do not want to speak.
- responding to a short e-mail from someone who thinks you are "God's gift to our church."
- responding to a long e-mail from someone who thinks the church is "losing its way."
- ignoring the pleas of the chair of the missions subcommittee who wants you to help prepare her report to the missions committee.
- calming the head usher who wants to know why teenage girls "in really short skirts and flip flops—I swear they were flip flops" are taking up the offering.
- hitting the snooze button next Sunday morning while thinking, "This would be such a good day to be a pagan."

Pastors can feel like traffic cops—standing in the middle of a busy intersection, at times just pretending to direct traffic, dodging cars, and wondering if at some point they will get run over. Sometimes being a minister is like nailing Jell-O to a tree without a hammer, herding cats without a horse, or working as a middle school assistant principal without the threat of detention.

Every church is Garrison Keillor's "Our Lady of Perpetual Responsibility." Ministers need a schedule grid like the ones in *TV Guide*. On Friday afternoon, every minister understands why the "Future Ministers of America Club" meets in a broom closet.

In recent surveys, ministers receive less respect than out-of-work rappers, people who put the plastic ends on shoestrings, and Harry Potter look-alikes. When people ask, "What do you do for a living?" I usually say, "I was an accountant at Enron," because it's easier to defend. "Clergy" sounds like the eighth dwarf—the one following "Sleepy." The *Jobs Rated Almanac* ranks minister thirty spots behind accountant, twenty spots behind parole officer, and ten behind the guy at the circus with the shovel. When experts talk about the "hot jobs of the future," gene programmers, pharmaceutical farmers, data miners, artificial intelligence brokers, and virtual reality actors make the list, but none of these occupations are close to ministry. Pastors show up on the "jobs of the past" list with stockbrokers, auto dealers, mail carriers, insurance agents, realtors, stenographers, and Democratic presidents.

After those Sundays when ministers are driven to check the classified ads, we discover that the life of ministry has left us unqualified for honest work. Ministers are not good at automotive repair, carpet cleaning, clerical help, construction work, customer service, or nightclub dancing. When ministers consider getting a "real" job, they quickly learn that none of these jobs are open to ministers. Employment counselors will not return your call. Careerfinders.com will not respond to your e-mails.

As a result, too many dull people get trapped in the ministry. Pastors, those reading this book excepted, can be boring. As a group, we are not the shiniest Krispy Kremes in the box. We might initially assume that people go into the ministry because they are already dull, as evidenced by many of our friends at seminary, but more often churches push their ministers into boredom. The squeaky wheels steal the grease, and ministers end up doing what's dull and expected.

So what do ministers do when we get sick of churches that have forgotten it's supposed to be fun? How do we respond when we are frustrated that the church isn't what it should be? Why is the church such a bureaucracy? Why is the church so afraid of risk? Why isn't the church more like Jesus?

When we feel burned out, we usually lower our expectations, walk away for a while, or stay irritated, but there's a better option than giving up or giving in.

The Westminster Catechism was written for ministers who have been "baited and switched" out of their primary work: "What is the chief work of human beings? To love God and enjoy God forever."

We always have the choice of enjoying God. Normal people don't work at a church; the ministry is a peculiar though glorious way to make a living. God helps us laugh at the ridiculous and celebrate the holy.

We can stop making the ministry less fun than it's supposed to be. The pay can be low and the hours are long, but the work is fascinating. The dullest day you've had as a minister is more interesting than the best day in most other professions. Pastors get to be generalists in a world filled with bored specialists. A minister is a priest, prophet, typist, bookworm, journalist, reformer, evangelist, counselor, fundraiser, community leader, public relations expert, master of ceremonies, professional tea-sipper and punch-drinker. Ministers get to be everywhere—preaching in worship, listening in meetings, teaching a class, marrying young lovers, waiting in maternity wards, praying with the sick, and burying the dead. We are always hip-deep in life. Ministers should love being ministers because the work gives our lives meaning. Who could ask for more?

Ministers should embrace the kind of humor that keeps us from being co-opted by what's most mundane in the system. Pastors can live more God-directed than church-directed. Ministry can be almost as good in practice as it is in principle. Church is wonderful, ridiculous, committed, superficial, robust, and trivial. If we acknowledge the church's shortcomings as well as our own, then we will smile at almost all of what makes it the church.

Ministers get lots of instruction on how to be a minister—books abound on small groups, evangelism, missions, and opening wallets wider. In *As Good as It Gets*, Jack Nicholson's character says, "I'm drowning here and you're describing the water." Most books on ministry describe the water. I wrote this book because I could use a book on how to *enjoy* being a minister.

My cynical friends have suggested that a book on the joy of ministry should be short—like "Deep Thoughts" by the cast of *Survivor*. None of the suggestions included in this book are guaranteed. Much of this is silly, but all of it is offered in the hope that ministers will reduce their stress by seeing with perspective, distinguishing the urgent from the genuinely important, and cultivating a life shaped by Christ's joy.

This book would not have been possible without the help of the saints and sinners who humored the pastor at: Mother Neff Baptist

Church, Moody, Texas (small church that no longer exists, but it's not the author's fault); Central Baptist Church, Paoli, Indiana (still exists, upright piano, hard-working farmers); College Heights Baptist Church, Manhattan, Kansas (still exists, funeral home quality organ, Kansas State professors); Lake Shore Baptist Church, Waco, Texas (still exists, small organ, Baylor University professors); Broadway Baptist Church, Fort Worth, Texas (still exists, big pipe organ, lots of lawyers).

Each of these churches is filled with people who laugh when it's funny. They taught me to do the same.

Writing a book that could be of incalculable value to clueless ministers was a delightful experience. Every minister should share whatever keys to sanity he or she has stumbled upon. Noted theologian/lyricist Jimmy Buffett sings for all ministers, "with all of our running and all of our cunning, If we couldn't laugh we would all go insane."

I'm Not Sure Who's Calling, but It's for You

When I was in eighth grade, an evangelist came to our church for a weeklong revival and offered the same lengthy invitation each night: "If you are not a Christian, then you need to come to the front, make a profession of faith, and become a Christian right now. If you are a Christian but have strayed into sin, then you need to come and rededicate your life. If you are a Christian and feel God tugging at your heart, then God is calling you to come to give yourself to full-time Christian service."

The evangelist was not easily dissuaded, so each night people went to the front to make decisions. By Thursday, the ones in my youth group who had not made some kind of decision were beginning to look suspect. I was already a Christian. I had been baptized when I was eight and had not strayed into sin. Some of my friends had started to stray into sin, but none of them had invited me to join them yet. I figured the tug on my heart must be a call to full-time Christian service. It sounded right. Part-time Christian service didn't seem like much of a commitment. I thought about it, prayed about it, talked to my parents (who took this way too seriously), wondered whether I could find institutions that would pay me to seek God's will, and made a public decision to give my full-time, whole life to God.

I made this decision with fear and trembling because I sincerely believed that I was opening myself up to all kinds of trouble. I imagined I would end up as a missionary to an uncharted island in the Pacific Ocean. My assignment would be to take the gospel to a tribe of sun-worshiping cannibals. I would row ashore in my canoe, tell the native women to wear shirts, lead them down "The Roman Road," and be taken to the chief. He would say, "Missionary, if you renounce Jesus" (I always imagined the chief speaking English), "then we will let you go home to your refrigerator, recliner, and televised sports, but if you insist on believing, then we will throw you into this huge kettle of boiling water and have you for our main course." The drums would stop pounding. The natives would stop chanting. The birds would stop singing. My heart would almost stop beating, but then it would pound as I, much like Martin Luther, defiantly said, "When I was in eighth grade I promised to die for what I believe. Throw another log on the fire." The story of my martyrdom would be in *Guideposts* and *Christianity Today*, and later condensed in *Reader's Digest*.

None of that has happened yet, but I'm only forty-three. Most days my heart doesn't pound with excitement. I haven't been mentioned in *Guideposts* or *Christianity Today* or known much of the drama that gets condensed in *Reader's Digest*. Looking back, the evangelist should have said, "If you are uninterested in fame, money, and sanity, you may want to consider becoming a minister."

Jerusalem

Like many ministers-in-waiting, I grew up in churches that had all the answers. Heaven was up, hell was down, and we knew who was going in which direction. God created the world in 6 days—144 hours. The Red Sea parted just like in the movie. Joshua made the sun stand still. The whale swallowed Jonah. If the Bible said Jonah swallowed the whale, we would have made that a test of faith. We took almost everything in the Bible literally—though not always seriously. We reduced the mystery of the Unknowable God to Four Spiritual Laws that would fit on a postcard and still leave room for "The Bible says it. I believe it. That settles it." We didn't have room for questions because we were certain of everything.

When I was a sophomore in high school, Eric, a senior, let me sit by him on the bus because I never pointed out how embarrassing it must be to be the only senior who couldn't find a less humiliating way to get home than riding the bus. Every afternoon, Monday through Friday, we discussed the problems of the world with the clarity that only teenagers can muster. Then one afternoon I made a casual, but likely insightful, reference to God. Eric replied—and nothing prepared me for this—"I don't believe in God."

"I'm sorry. I must have misunderstood. What did you say?"

"I don't believe in God. My parents don't either. God just doesn't make sense."

As a budding young theologian, you might guess that I responded, "In the thirteenth century, in his *Summa Theologiae*, St. Thomas Aquinas offered five ontological proofs for the existence of God; let's talk about each one of them," but I was too stunned to speak. I looked carefully to see if there was something about Eric I had not noticed before—pointed ears or missing pupils. When you meet your first atheist you expect him to be carrying a gun, a bottle of whiskey, a Ouija board, something. I was raised, like most ministerial larvae, in a small world.

If I was going to be a Baptist minister, then I had to go to a Baptist university. I chose Baylor University, Jerusalem on the Brazos, because I thought of it as a bastion of liberalism that needed me to straighten out its misguided freethinkers. If the Bible said, "Thus saith the Lord," then the professors better act like "thus saith the Lord" or they would have to answer to one angry freshman. My first religion class was Introduction to Old Testament. I hadn't figured out that college students don't read the assigned text, so after the first day of class I read the first 100 pages of Bernard Anderson's *Understanding the Old Testament*. In his commentary on Noah and the flood, one line set my blood boiling. Anderson wrote that the closing of the ark by the hand of God was a "naïve anthropomorphic touch." I wasn't sure what a "naïve anthropomorphic touch" was, but I knew my home church wouldn't approve. I underlined the offensive passage, made several exclamation points in the margin, and marched out of the library to begin the crusade by straightening out Dr. C. W. Christian, the heretical professor who had assigned the profane textbook. I began calmly, but firmly: "Dr. Christian, you may not realize that the textbook you assigned questions the Word of God. Here on page ninety-eight it says that in Genesis, which was written by Moses as I hope you know, when we read that God closed the door of the ark, that is a 'naïve anthropomorphic touch.' I'm not positive what that means, but it doesn't sound like a compliment. I don't think we should question the Bible."

Dr. Christian, who is aptly named, gently replied, "Do you think God might want us to ask questions about the Bible? Could it be that God wants us to work to believe? Maybe faith shouldn't be easy."

It was the beginning of the end and the beginning of the beginning. By the conclusion of our conversation, it was obvious even to a state Bible drill champion (Mississippi, 1971) that there was more real belief in his questions than in my answers. For better and worse, I transferred my ministerial aspirations from the church of the certain to the church of the questioning. Becoming a minister would mean wrestling with doubts, faith, despair, and joy.

Non-Amish Women in Tight-fitting Jeans

The struggles ahead weren't only theological. My parents, my church, and most of my friends called themselves Baptist, but in reality we were, in most of the ways that mattered to a teenager, Amish. We not only didn't drink or sleep around, but we didn't know anyone who did. We saw those people. They went to the grocery store that sold beer. Everyone at our church went to the store that didn't sell beer. We knew where the pool hall was, where most of the drinking reportedly took place, but no one in my youth group had ever been through the door. Not only had alcohol never passed my lips, but I had never seen it pass anyone else's lips either. We knew there were seventeen-year-olds who slept around, but we didn't know any of them—though I tended to imagine such women wearing bright red dresses or tight-fitting blue jeans. They had long painted fingernails and were looking for young Baptist/Amish victims to lure into depravity. (The Amish kids were less sheltered than I was.)

Before I went to Baylor, a deacon concerned that I was going some place more worldly than Bob Jones University pulled me aside and said, "When you get to college, you will face temptations that you have never imagined. There will be hard-drinking, loose-living women. You need to decide right now that you will have nothing to do with them, because if the devil gets hold of you, she doesn't let go."

As a freshman I was constantly on the lookout out for wild women with drinking problems, but I couldn't find any. After a while I let my guard down. While taking Introduction to New Testament I was distracted by a Lutheran pastor's daughter who sat in front of me. Yvonne was attractive enough to frighten me, but she seemed like a nice person. After a couple of weeks she said, "Hi," and I said, "Hi." I was thrilled that we were hitting it off. After a few more weeks of waiting for her to say "Hi" again, I finally asked if she would like to go out to eat and to a G-rated movie. We went to a nice family-friendly Mexican restaurant. We talked about our churches and how wonderful it is to be a preacher's kid, but when our food came, she said—and I'll never forget this, though I tried—"Isn't it strange to have Mexican food without beer?" I tried to keep breathing but couldn't. She might as well have said, "Isn't it strange to eat enchiladas without crack cocaine sprinkled on top?"

I realized who she was. She was temptation. The devil had arrived and she was wearing blue jeans. She was a hard-drinking, loose-living woman planning to lure me into the depravity that I had been warned about.

I spent the rest of the evening terrified, but apparently she recognized my spiritual strength and the invisible armor of God I was wearing and, to my disappointment, made no further attempts to steal my soul.

What I've learned since then, also to my disappointment, is that for most ministers temptation doesn't wear a red dress or tight-fitting blue jeans. The temptations most likely to steal ministerial souls are quiet and boring. The temptations are to be dull and apathetic, and they are more dangerous than I ever imagined.

Will This Be on the Test?

If you're lucky, your preparation for ministry includes as many years as you can stay at a scintillating seminary or divinity school. A gifted, caring faculty will teach you and other ministerial students with heavy briefcases so much that you will soon forget.

What do ministers remember years later? If the average seminary student shared what he or she recalls ten years after graduation, their responses might look something like this:

- *Chapel*—Most students don't have chapel memories. Seminaries provide chapel so that future ministers will understand people who skip worship.
- *Christian classics*—Augustine felt really guilty and took way too many pages writing about it. Brother Lawrence loved working in the kitchen. He was Julia Child on Prozac. Teresa of Avila, meanwhile, could have used stronger medication.

- *Christian education*—Whatever the topic, form small groups, then share what you discussed with the large group.
- *Church and community*—Inner-city churches have a hard time. Suburban ministry requires a willingness to play golf.
- *Church history*—There were so many early councils (conventions without exhibits) that they ran together even for the expense accounters who attended them. The Reformation began when Martin Luther nailed ninety-five strong suggestions to an expensive church door and left an unattractive nail hole. During the First Great Awakening, many Americans stopped sleeping in church. During the Second Great Awakening, their children woke up.
- *Counseling*—"How does that make you feel?" is an acceptable question. "What do you think I'm feeling?" is not.
- *Denominational heritage*—The church splintered into little pieces, but our denomination (the one that owns your seminary) held Jesus' view. Most denominations share what they think of as their denomination's distinctives.
- *Ethics*—There are at least two sides to every argument, so listen carefully before telling people on the other side why they are wrong.
- *Evangelism*—Program evangelism doesn't work. In every church, there are three people, two of whom are married to each other, who will never admit this.
- *Greek*—There are three New Testament words for love—*phileo* (fraternal love), *agape* (self-giving love), and *eros* (love outside the church).
- *Hebrew*—Hebrew is read right to left. This makes not remembering any Hebrew more excusable.
- *Leadership*—Ask smart people to chair committees. Ignore difficult people.
- *Missions*—The goal of early missionaries was to convince people in other cultures to go to Bible study on Sunday at 9:30 and to worship at 11:00. The invention of the slide projector created the additional responsibility of taking pictures. Conservative seminar-

ies encourage missionaries to "Tell!" while liberal seminaries encourage missionaries to "Listen!"

- *New Testament*—The Synoptics were Matthew, Mark, and Luke. John wanted to be a Synoptic but was at least twenty years too late. Phylacteries aren't what they sound like. Revelation is a mystery. Canonization was the process by which publishers decided how many pages the Bible should be. Some could have skipped the twenty pages of mystery at the end.
- *Old Testament*—The Pentateuch, the highest point of the temple, was written by four friends nicknamed J, E, P, and D. Isaac means laughter, but after his dad pulled out the meat cleaver, Isaac almost never laughed. Nefretiri, Anne Baxter in *The Ten Commandments*, is disappointingly a figment of Cecil B. Demille's imagination. In the book of Ruth we read, "Ruth came softly and uncovered his feet and laid her down. . . . And Ruth said, 'Spread therefore thy skirt over thine handmaid.'" Don't speculate on what this means.
- *Pastoral care*—Don't sit on the hospital bed. Never say a prayer just to end a visit—unless it's the only way to get out of the room.
- *Philosophy*—Philosophy is really complicated.
- *Preaching*—Sermon preparation is the act of discovering the three points found in every passage of Scripture.
- *Theology*—Karl Barth was a heretic, a genius, pushy, or all of the above. Eschatology is what happens at the end. Say, "I'm a pan-millennialist—it will all pan out in the end." It's never been a funny joke, but it's easier than explaining the other choices.

Mark Twain argued that education is what's left after we've forgotten the facts. Let's hope he was right. Even if we remembered all of it, we would leave seminary with a wonderful lack of understanding of how much we don't know. We might be surprised to learn that most days the Post-Nicene Fathers don't enter ministers' thinking.

The bigger questions that seminary raises are often "Do we still love God or are we too sophisticated?" "Does a professional degree disqualify us from having any fun?" "Will we find that it's easier to look intelligent than it is to follow Christ?"

At seminary, the black and white absolutes melt into a fuzzy gray. Students learn enough Greek to know that translating Jesus' words takes a surprising amount of guessing; enough redaction criticism to see that Matthew, Mark, Luke, and John aren't always talking about the same Jesus; enough historical criticism to wonder if Paul would recognize Jesus if he saw him on the street; enough of Rudolph Bultmann's Christology to know that Rudolph Bultmann and Christology are both tricky; enough soteriology to recognize that saying who's in and who's out isn't as simple as it was in Mrs. Dot Dailey's third grade Sunday school class; enough church history to know that the votes at the councils that wrote the creeds were as confused as a television preacher at the Jesus seminar. It gets harder to say "true God from true God, begotten not made, of one being with the Father" without wanting to raise your hand to ask questions. This sense of bewilderment is the perfect preparation for the ministry.

Exactly Why Did the Last Pastor Leave?

While at seminary, students learn to dream of the perfect church. In these fantasy congregations, ministers hear:

"The sanctuary must be getting smaller because I can never get a seat near the front."

"We're going to have to stiffen the qualifications for Sunday school teachers again. We have too many volunteers."

"Pastor, a friend of mine works at Smyth & Helwys Publishing. Would you mind if I put some of your sermons together and sent a proposal?"

"You need a break, Pastor. Instead of the convention, why don't we send you to a resort in the Bahamas?"

"Since we're so much over budget, why don't we give the pastor a big Christmas bonus?"

What ministers don't realize is that churches dream of the perfect pastor. The ideal preacher will agree with every member on everything and challenge everybody else to change their minds. The flawless shepherd will be at church from eight in the morning until nine at night, attend every meeting, and have plenty of time for picnics with the family. The complete cleric will know Hebrew and Greek but never mention either—no big fat Greek sermons. The model minister is twenty-seven years old and has preached thirty-five years, has a burning desire to work with teenagers, and plays the piano at the nursing home. He or she is a younger, hipper, more 007 version of the last minister, with all of the qualities and none of the imperfections, all of the wisdom plus all of the energy expended acquiring that wisdom.

A few churches are waiting for a minister to be their genial cruise director, but most expect the pastor to set the woods on fire. The minister will bring the dead church to life. Inspiring preaching will awaken them from spiritual inertia, lead them to forsake ungodly apathy, and transform the community into Mitford.

The bizarre expectations on both sides make choosing and being chosen by a church an odd as well as deadly serious business. Many ministers who wish they weren't ministers actually wish they weren't ministers with bad congregations. Pastors are at the mercy of those with whom they serve. No church leaves a minister unchanged or unscarred, for better or worse, richer or poorer, in sickness or in health.

This Swimsuit Makes My Hips Look Big

Systems for matching shepherds and sheep range from organized, reasonable arrangements to the nonsensical Baptist system with which I am most familiar.

Search committees try to convince their congregations that their process for finding a pastor makes perfect sense. They will listen to church members' ideas no matter how peculiar, collect resumes, hear enough sermons to make them wonder why they agreed to be on the search committee, talk to the prospective pastor (polite version), talk to references (Why would her own mother call her unreliable?), talk to the prospective pastor again (grueling version), do a credit check, do a criminal check, do a polygraph, send the prospective pastor hundreds of pages of information, talk to the prospective pastor again (every card on the table), and invite the prospective pastor to visit the church of every minister's dreams.

From the perspective of the searched, the process is not nearly so organized. Your first formal contact comes in a letter that begins, "You may be a winner. I am writing on behalf of our Pastor Search Committee. We have been given your name . . . ." You are to write in response, "Thank you for your recent inquiry. I have great admiration for your church's tradition of worship and ministry." (Most write this even if they have never heard of the church.)

The scores for preliminary rounds are thrown out as soon as you advance to meeting with the committee. The question-and-answer is always more important than the swimsuit competition, though it may not feel like it.

One popular strategy, particularly with ministers with something to hide, is to take the offensive and ask lots of questions. You can impress a search committee with poignant queries. Such questions identify you as a minister with a grasp of issues concerning search committees, congregational life, and church administration:

- Is the rest of the church as smart as this committee?
- Was this committee chosen by throwing dice? Were you the winners?
- Have you been repeatedly turned down by pastors less qualified than I am?
- Will you be checking into my personal finances? Could I check into your personal finances?
- Is the criminal background check negotiable?
- Who would you rather have as your pastor—Jerry Springer, Barbara Walters, or Regis Philbin? (If they choose Jerry, end the interview. If they ask whom you're most like, go with Oprah.)
- Why did the last pastor leave? Is the last pastor still institutionalized?

- To what year in your church's history are you trying to get back?
- How would you feel about your church getting significantly smaller?
- Who would you like to see the pastor fire?
- Who else could the pastor fire?
- What's the most infuriating thing the pastor's secretary does?
- Does the pastor run staff meetings? Does the pastor attend staff meetings?
- How many hours do you think your pastor should work? Are you serious?
- How often do you have business meetings? Are you sure that's wise?
- How many committees do you have? Could we halve that number?
- How many deacons do you have? Could we halve that number?
- Will psychological help be available?

By the time you have gotten the answers you desire, the committee will beg you to be their supreme spiritual guide. Don't let their adoration keep you from looking critically at their church. Keep listening for danger signals. Comments like "We've been looking for someone for so long" should frighten you. Don't stop asking questions. If the church budget is printed in red, ask about it. If you notice a gun rack in the pastor's study, ask about it. If most of the last names in the church directory are the same, ask about it.

Be open to positive signs. Ask about the last pastor. The pastor you want to follow is lazy, long-winded, and a poor dresser. I once followed a minister who wore Hawaiian shirts and shorts to the office. I will never be able to thank him enough.

Know that a committee's assurance that "We'll have that taken care of before the new pastor arrives" means "This will be your first headache."

Sometimes it's easy to decide whether to accept a church's invitation ("I'll go upstairs and pray about it. You pack the bags."), but most of the time, it's hope for the Spirit and make an educated guess.

Just a Little More, Sir

Once you've said "I do," the process gets more ridiculous. You immediately shift from the anointed one to an employee with job-related injuries on the way. Ministers negotiate dental with the very congregants they must inspire. There should be ministerial agents who negotiate for pastors who don't have any idea what FICA stands for, but I haven't been able to locate them.

Pastors in free church traditions, who should have formed unions long ago, get thrown to finance and personnel committees like shepherds to wolves. These questions for the negotiating phase will be as tremendously helpful as the earlier questions suggested for the search committee phase:

• Is this less than the last pastor made? Will I be expected to do less work?
• Will I get as much vacation, retirement, and health insurance as you do at your place of work?
• Is the Sabbatical program as nonexistent as I'm guessing it is?
• If I go over the allotted mileage reimbursement, should I stop visiting people in the hospital?
• What should I do if I want to buy more than three books this year?
• What about a reimbursement to cover Girl Scout cookies?
• Is there a job description for the pastor? Is it filled with lies?
• Could I please have some more, sir? Please.

Don't feel bad about asking for a living wage. Someone noticing that you are underpaid is as likely as Eminem starring in the next *Left Behind* movie. The list of church members to whom the minister may later complain without looking greedy can be engraved on a grain of rice. Once you're through the negotiating stage, you can start being Christian again.

Swearing Not to Litter

Before I got to Broadway Baptist Church, the first graders made a list of qualifications/demands for their new pastor. They wrote them in red, green, and purple magic markers on two big sheets of manila paper and importunately taped their overly ambitious catalog to the door of their Sunday school room. I remain to this day quite intimidated. I couldn't claim to have the credentials they insisted upon, but felt like I should respond in the church newsletter—especially since there were no first graders on the Search Committee.

Not to litter—This is a very good requirement with which to start. I would not want a pastor who litters. I promise not to litter.

Not do drugs—This is even worse than littering. I promise not to do drugs.

Love God—This is a great suggestion. If Jesus were making this list, I think this would be first.

Love Jesus—Lots of ministers forget this one. I'll try to remember.

Love the world—I will try to love the parts that God loves and be sad about the parts that make God sad.

Take care of our people—I look forward to caring for the people at our church. I know that we will all take care of each other.

A girl pastor—It's a great idea. I'm sorry. I promise to encourage girls to be pastors of other churches.

A young pastor—I look pretty old to six-year-olds, but I'll try to be young at heart.

Someone who does not show off—When I was a first grader my mother thought I had a problem with this one, but I'm getting better about it.

Be kind to everyone—This is asking a lot, but I'll try.

Be kind to other people—Somehow this sounds more realistic.

Love children—My two children remind me of how much fun it is to love children.

Love nature—I don't like poison ivy or fire ants, but I like almost everything else.

Love animals—We have a fish named Stripe, but that's it. I love Bugs Bunny. Does that count?

Answer our questions—I would love to hear your questions and answer the ones I can answer. Your list makes me think that you have some great answers of your own.

Love with hope—This is one of the best descriptions of what a pastor should do that I have ever heard. I will try to remember, and you can remind me, that my job is to love with hope.

Adventures in Moving

"Loving with hope" is more spiritual than "having to move." The ordeal of moving is one of the best reasons to be absolutely sure before you take a job that isn't in your neighborhood.

"Moving Day" has all the appeal of "Income Tax Day" or "Pledge Sunday." I like to have Mayflower move us, because it's honest to name your moving company after a long, miserable trip on which everyone got sick.

The first step is to box the books you had to buy to get through seminary (far more books than you have read). On the first day of moving, pack your books alternating spines up and down as described in *Moving Tips: Everything You Want to Know About a Truly Dismal Process*. Books should be carefully and lovingly divided into church history, ethics, counseling, etc. On the second day of moving, toss books into boxes marked "church office, miscellaneous."

When you unpack, the most singularly embarrassing event in the life cycle, your new church members will come to see that you have thrown Bibles into a Johnny Walker box.

On the first day at your new home, you will unpack carefully. By the second day, you will pour boxes out on the floor. Church members will bring cookies, but they will not know how to keep vertical blinds vertical.

On your third day the washer will explode. Water will pour out of a pipe in the back. You will mop, sweep, and survey the damage. While you normally make some attempt at appearing mechanically inclined at such mishaps, you won't even pretend to be able to fix such a major problem. When the repairperson comes, he or she will take the offending pipe, which will actually be a tube, out of the back of the washer and place it into the drainage pipe. It will take five seconds. A merciful machinist will give a short, seemingly heart-felt speech on bright people who aren't mechanically inclined. Appreciate the attempt at kindness, but recognize it as pity.

The act of moving is a gift of God to remind ministers of how incredibly dependent we are. During the horror of moving, you will depend on some combination of packers, cleaners, movers, real-tors, friends, family, and friends who will become family. The humiliation involved makes moving a fine way to begin a ministry.

Keys to Success

Nothing beats the euphoria you feel the first time you see your name on the sign in front of the church in semi-durable vinyl letter-ing, but it quickly gives way to the feeling that you have walked into the wrong class—church administration instead of the New Testament Greek for which you studied. Everyone else knows the answers. There are names, dates, and stories for which they only use the punch line: "We know not to let Marge fix the communion bread. Ha! Ha!" The confused minister is left to smile stupidly, having no idea what's going on. Of course, people who want to help are waiting outside your door. Some of the first ones to seek you out have agendas, pet peeves, a thirst for power, and the scalp of the last pastor in their trunk. Do not let the big kids throw you into the deep water.

When you move to a new church, it's a chance for the new people to think you're smarter and more together than you really are—or at least smarter and more together than the people where you used to live thought you were. Moving to a new church is a chance to leave behind every time you've spilled tea, mispronounced a name, or lost your keys.

A week after arriving at my present church, I got out of Ben Johnson's Toyota Forerunner. Ben, a high school student at my new church, had graciously loaned me his car. (It may have been his parents that offered the car; that's unclear.) On Sunday morning, I locked the car door and walked into the church. I decided to leave most of my keys in the desk, but carefully took the office key—in case the door was locked when I came back. (I'm a careful person.) After worship, I went by the Committee on Committees meeting long enough to justify eating their pizza and suggest a Committee on the Committee on Committees. When I returned to the aforementioned Forerunner, I had every key except one. This was confusing, because I'm a careful person. I checked the key ring ten times. I looked under the car. I walked slowly back to my office staring at the pavement, the floor, the stairs. I emptied my pockets and turned them inside out.

I finally had to admit that I had to admit to one of the new people—one of the ones I hoped would think I'm smart—that I had lost the key. I called the Johnsons and explained that I am a careful person, but something mysterious, almost unbelievable, had happened and their key was missing. There was no need for this to be blown out of proportion or for anybody else to hear about it. Cindy, Ben's mother, said that she would talk to Roland, Ben's father, and that I should talk to Ben, who was at the church. Now at least three people were going to think that I am the kind of person who loses car keys—which I am not. I found Ben just as choir practice ended: "Ben, you don't know me that well, but I'm not the kind of person who loses car keys. Nonetheless, in this baffling world unexplainable things happen. Please tell me that you have a key to your car and end my shame." Ben thought there might be one at home. I began to believe that an intruder had stolen the key. Ben later called to say that I had lost the only key in existence.

On Monday morning, I realized that I would now have to beg for rides and explain to other people that I lost the key. At staff meeting, the minister of youth suggested that I "retrace my steps"—a helpful, insulting suggestion. I retraced my steps and found the key underneath my desk where, apparently, an intruder had kicked it.

I thought about this episode too much and decided that I am, after all, the kind of minister who loses car keys. I was wrong to hide my lack of togetherness. Ministers need to admit that we lose our keys. One of the basic requirements to be the church is to admit that we aren't as smart and together as we wish. Being lost is how we all get to church.

Habits of Highly Effective Ministers

Within the first month at your new church, present your goals and objectives for the coming year. This should be a dull list:

Earnest, Yet Uninteresting Goals and Objectives

(1) To get moved in, adequately set up, and organized to serve God in the office. I will make appointments in the morning and reserve the afternoon for preparation for worship, preaching, and Bible study. (This will never happen, but it makes you sound smart.)

(2) To lead worship and preach sermons that will challenge people in the discipleship of Christian living. (At this point, they still believe they want to be "challenged.")

(3) To strengthen and enrich the partnership in my marriage and priority of my family. (Use this one only if you have a family. If you have children and are in a Democratic church, add, "I came to this church with the understanding that you will be the village that helps raise my children." If you're in a Republican church, add, "My

spouse and I take seriously our responsibility to raise our children without the help of any so-called village.")

(4) To create and set up patterns for well-being and growth for myself: private prayer, regular exercise, and creative study. (Interpret "creative study" as any movie without Adam Sandler.)

(5) To work in a healthy way toward completing my grief about leaving my last place of service. (Say this even if leaving your last place of service felt like escaping from Alcatraz.)

(6) To give support and pastoral care to the staff of the church. (Find out which staff members have résumés out and which ones should.)

(7) To get genuinely acquainted with people at the church. (The pictorial directory is misleading, but still an ally.)

(8) To understand the structure of the church ministry and organization. (Who died and made the finance committee king?)

Even as you present this dull, though earnest list, you are leaving out your real goals.

Goals and Objectives I Left Out

(1) To learn to drive around the city without a map on the dashboard.

(2) To be confident enough at setting the church alarm that I don't feel the need to run out the front door after the red light starts flashing and the beeping begins.

(3) To learn names. Especially the names of those who ask, "Do you know who I am?"

(4) To stay long enough to hear someone say "This is our pastor" rather than "This is our new pastor."

The Honeymooners

When people from other churches find out that you have only been at your new church for a short time they will often ask, "How is the honeymoon going?" They have recognized that pastors go through stages in their relationship to the church. The initial giddiness of "Oh, my! I can't wait until Sunday!" will, at times, give way to a more subdued "Oh my, it's almost Sunday."

Marriage experts (almost an oxymoron) have identified five stages of a healthy, deepening romance. In the first stage, you believe that your beloved is absolutely perfect. Your intended is everything you dreamed. The honeymoon is not, as you might guess, the lengthiest of stages. In the second phase, you discover that the love of your life is not perfect. There are a few tiny things about your sweetie that you would like to change, and so a gentle power struggle ensues as you go about correcting those minor flaws. In the third stage, you give up on remaking your partner. Your dearest can be a pain, but you promised "for better or worse." The fourth phase moves beyond acceptance to approval. The movement from the third to fourth stage is from stability to commitment. Only the most fortunate, dedicated couples ever get to the fifth stage— co-creativity. Couples help each other become more of what they should be and share with others from the overflow. They become a gift to the world—doing more good together than they ever could apart.

This way of looking at romance is not definitive. Most couples go through the stages several times. Spouses might spend time in five different stages in one day. Like many theories (especially theories on anything as ephemeral as romance), this one is partly truth and partly fiction.

Nevertheless, these stages of romance offer an imperfect analogy for ministerial romances with the church. At the beginning, pastors join a church and believe that they have found the completely flawless, just-what-God-intended congregation. The honeymoon is not, as you might guess, a lengthy stage. In the second phase we discover that the church is not perfect. There are things about our churches that we want to fix. (Why do we have a church council?) In the third stage, we give up on remaking our church into the church we have always imagined, and accept it as it is. (Ignore the finance committee and they will leave you alone.) The fourth stage moves beyond acceptance to gratitude. In this phase, we see the good gifts of our church and give thanks. The fifth stage, co-creativity, includes the most fortunate, dedicated ministers. Minister and church help one another become more of what they should be. The church romance becomes a gift to the world—doing more good together than they could ever do apart.

Enjoy the honeymoon—even if you feel like you got married without dating nearly enough. If you're lucky, you're discovering family members you never knew you had. Some members of your new church will be pains in the neck. Enjoy not knowing their names as long as you can. Even in the initial state of bliss we need to see not only that we will soon have "been there, done that" (and hopefully will be there and do that again), but that we will spend time in different stages, and learn to give thanks for them all.

(three)

I Scream Sundays

Two months after finishing the Master of Divinity degree, I became the pastor of Central Baptist Church, Paoli, Indiana—a city with three thousand people and three Baptist churches. The search committee said that 90 percent of my job was preaching three times a week—Sunday morning, Sunday night, and Wednesday night. I felt good about that because I thought I was a proficient preacher. I made A's in my homiletics courses at seminary. My mother said I had potential. You can imagine my astonishment to discover that the people in my new congregation were bored during my sermons (sermons that had, as I mentioned, received A's at seminary). Danny Freemyer, who sat on the second row, fell asleep every Sunday. He could make it through the hymns, but thirty seconds into my brilliant exposition of Holy Scripture he was out and loud enough for everyone within ten rows (the entire sanctuary) to hear. Claudine Marion, third row, chewed gum to drive out the sound of Danny snoring. Reid Hodges, a teenager, sat in the back under the balcony and read something that wasn't the Bible, cleverly hidden in the hymnal. Several choir members left after the "special music" each Sunday to help in the nursery, but the nursery workers they were ostensibly relieving never came into the sanctuary. One person,

Dave Wilkinson, initially gave me hope. He spent each sermon rifling through his Bible. I thought, "At least one person is thinking about what I'm saying." Then at the back of the sanctuary after worship one Sunday, I learned that Dave was listing verses to make it clear how misguided the preacher was. These nice people daydreamed, coughed, and glazed over during every sermon, because they had learned that preachers are boring.

Most sermons are dull because churches make their preachers dull. When we weren't paying attention, someone decided that the goal of the church is tranquility. Unlike the early days of Christianity, the church now serves people who think of themselves as "nice" and want to keep peace no matter how boring it might be.

John the Baptist would have lost his head sooner if he had been pastor of your church. Congregations find ways to let their preachers know which subjects are off limits. When pastor search committees say, "We want you to say whatever you believe," they mean, "You may say anything on which 95 percent of us agree, providing the remaining 5 percent are not big givers." It's not long before some leader in the church says, as nicely as possible, "We want you to say whatever God lays on your heart, but we are afraid that some subjects might get in the way of your ministry. We want you to stay here a long time, so you may want to avoid abortion, euthanasia, gambling, cloning, the environment, affirmative action, capital punishment, the Middle East, the Pope, George Bush, the Osbournes, and the unimportance of professional football."

Some churches have self-appointed thorns in the flesh. At one church I served, there was a nice gentleman—I'll call him "Darth Vader" (his real name is Javert)—who helpfully presented a list of subjects on which my opinions were no longer of interest to him or those whom he represented. I explained to Mr. Vader that if I no longer addressed politics, hunger, racism, ecumenicity, the equality of women, the relationship between Christianity and other religions, the inclusiveness of the gospel, the centrality of grace, the radical nature of Jesus' ministry, or God, I wouldn't have much left to say.

Preachers repeat conventional ideas with which everyone agrees because they have been told not to rock the boat. The White House press secretary, spokespeople for the tobacco industry, and undercover spies have more freedom to tell the truth than most ministers. Too many pastors act as if George Gallup helped them find out which topics are acceptable. An imaginary "How am I preaching? Call the church office" sticker is on the front of the pulpit. These cowardly pastors later confide to other ministers:

"I wonder what our congregation would do if I said what I really think."

"When I find a place to move, I've got a ten-point sermon I've been saving."

"My favorite Bible story is the one where snakes bite half of Moses' congregation."

Dull pastors are like bank tellers who can't count—they make everyone in the profession look bad—but their approach is understandable. Conventional, uninteresting preachers have good reasons to avoid unconventional, interesting ideas. Years of ministry have left us with a startling lack of knowledge of most things that are interesting. At our worst, pastors end up affirming dull platitudes because we don't want to spend Monday morning answering angry e-mails or lose our ability to pay the light bill. At our best, we love God and our congregations enough to risk it.

Ministers preach the truth because it keeps their souls alive. If we only preach what's expected and ignore our conscience, we might as well be working in wedding chapels in Las Vegas.

We need to talk about homosexuality, materialism, militarism, ecology, sexism, pluralism, evangelism, and why the Episcopalians have more money. We need to preach about hopes, dreams, and the Spirit or we'll forget our hopes and dreams and never feel the Spirit.

A Brief Aside for Angry Prophets

This section on courageous preaching is not meant for that minority of ministers who light up when anything controversial comes up. A few pastors relish the blood of conflict. Stephen is their model for preaching. They have "When they heard this, all in the synagogue were filled with fury—Luke 4:28" cross-stitched and hanging in their study. If nobody is mad, then they figure they must not be doing their jobs. These are not normal ministers. I can't imagine that any of them are reading this book.

What I Meant to Say

We know how to preach the truth. What we want to know is how to keep our jobs while doing so. How do we experience the joy of saying what we need to say instead of the dullness of saying what they expect to hear? I have preached on controversial issues and kept my job—at least the one I have right now—and so here are one's pastor's wild guesses.

How to Preach the Truth without Losing
Your Job or Soul

(1) *Launch a preemptive strike:* This has to take place before you've said anything on which anyone could disagree. Shortly after getting to a new church, say something like this from the pulpit: "I am delighted to be part of a congregation where no one has suggested what I should not preach. This church encourages, challenges, and requires its pastor to think, ask questions, voice doubts, and dream new dreams. As a church you have learned how good it is to have minds and hearts open enough to celebrate our rich diversity. Ours is not a melting pot of ideas but a glorious mosaic of thought. For a pastor, there are few gifts so cherished as the freedom to seek truth

wherever it may be found. I recognize how fortunate I am to be part of this thinking, loving, gracious church."

I waited too long to say this to my present congregation—a week.

(2) *Introduce controversial sermons in a low-key way*: "If you're carrying any blunt instruments, please pass them to the ushers."

(3) *Mean what you say*: "It may seem ironic that I am preaching on the ninth commandment after IRS agents came by my office this week."

(4) *Blame Jesus*: "What was Jesus thinking? I don't like this 'love your enemies' stuff any more than you do. It's a good thing Jesus isn't President."

(5) *Don't go negative.* Use positive images: "Wouldn't it be great if every starving, poverty-stricken child ate as well as they do in the congressional cafeteria?"

(6) *Tell sweet stories*: "Then the hungry child said, 'Are you Jesus?' I answered, 'No, but I'm one of his friends.'"

(7) *Use humor*: "Ever since that fateful day in 1924 when John Thomas Scopes told his principal that he would rather teach biology than driver's ed, pastors haven't known how to talk about evolution."

(8) *Bring controversial questions into the congregation's everyday life*: "Imagine for a moment that your pastor is gay." (This is not a good suggestion for every congregation.)

(9) *Share cold, hard facts*: "Studies show that your pastor is right most of the time."

(10) *Speak openly and honestly about your own struggles with the topic*: "I used to be wrong about this, too."

(11) *Make a forthright statement of your own viewpoint on the subject*: "Forget what I just said. I keep changing my mind. I don't know what to think."

(12) *Present all sides of the issue fairly*: "I suppose there could be a bright person on the other side of this issue, though I don't see how."

(13) *Avoid deriding and inflammatory language*: "I'm not saying the other viewpoint is the stupidest thing I've ever heard."

(14) *Preach with a realistic expectation for the sermon*: "Put your lottery tickets in the offering plate."

(15) *Articulate questions for the listener*: "You're wondering, 'How can my preacher be so smart?'"

(16) *Flirt with heresy every once in a while.* Every preacher needs to stand at the sanctuary door shaking hands and saying, "I'm sorry if I hurt your feelings." Someone I should footnote said that the catcher is Jesus, the batter is the congregation, and the preacher is not to shake off the sign. Make it hard to hit, but throw it over the plate.

Sermons on the Amount

In the pursuit of joy in ministry, few categories require as much creativity and special attention as preaching on stewardship. If you only cry during one sermon a year it should be the stewardship sermon. If you only cry before one sermon a year it should be the stewardship sermon. Most churches have an annual stewardship campaign—a time for church members to think prayerfully about the way in which they share financially the work of the church. At our church during the week before Pledge Sunday, the stewardship committee mails every member what is, with the possible exception of income tax refunds, the most anticipated mail of the year—the annual stewardship request and pledge card. This is the committee's way of saying, "Don't come to church this Sunday."

Ministers need to know the keys to effective stewardship: committing to stewardship year-round; talking openly about money; guiding programs by grace rather than guilt; not allowing the pastor to preach on Stewardship Sunday.

Catchy, corny sermon titles can make a stewardship campaign. "Money Talks, But It Lies," "Stewardships that Fail to Sail," and "Not Everyone Is Fit to Be Tithed" all say something incomprehensible.

Preachers traditionally begin stewardship sermons with subtle disclaimers:

"I don't like talking about this!"

"I don't talk about this very often!"

"I have to do this!"

"I'm not like other ministers who ask for money!"

As you think about the best way to pry away the bucks, er, share the joy of giving, consider presenting your sermon as a bad drama. The closing line could be a person with an empty wallet saying, "I'm sorry, Jesus. I spent it all. It's so hard to make ends meet these days. Would you like to ride my jet ski?"

The Bible has a great deal to say about stewardship:

• "God loves a cheerful giver" (2 Corinthians 9:7).
• "The love of money is the root of all evil" (1 Timothy 6:10).
• "Feasts are made for laughter; wine gladdens life, and money meets every need" (Ecclesiastes 10:19—That doesn't sound right. Forget that one.).
• "Now when Ananias heard these words, he fell down and died" (Acts 5:5—This is from my favorite stewardship story).

Pithy quotes on stewardship can be enlightening:

- "When I have money, I get rid of it quickly, lest it find a way into my heart." (John Wesley)
- "Each of us will one day be judged by our measure of giving—not by our measure of wealth." (William Arthur Ward)
- "A dead church doesn't ask for money." (Clara Bess Eikner)
- "I'd find the fellow who lost it, and if he was poor, I'd return it." (Yogi Berra—when asked what he would do on finding a million dollars in the street)

Avoid hard-sell obnoxious stewardship sermons, but toss out gentle threats like turning off the air conditioner or providing no coffee before Bible study.

Some of the most interesting stewardship sermons promise rewards for giving:

- "The more you give, the more you will get."
- "Tithing will make you irresistible to the opposite sex."
- "People who give to the church live longer." (If it's not true, it should be.)

These suggestions will help your stewardship sermon ring the registers. Ka-ching!

Strange Bedfellows

Every year, as the first Tuesday in November draws near, ministers grow increasingly confused about what's appropriate to say and what the IRS says isn't. Faith and politics is a minefield through which pastors tiptoe. Endorsing a particular candidate from the pulpit is clearly inappropriate unless one of the candidates is a wrestler or actor.

The best way to get away with talking about politics is to offer biblical ideas that will not be in either Democratic or Republican platforms. A national gleaning law, listening to your enemies, the elimination of national borders, and beating swords into plowshares may be in the Bible, but they won't make it into any stump speeches. Saying outlandish things no politician would claim is the easiest way to tell the truth and not get audited.

A Few Difficult Preaching Questions the Author Is Happy to Answer

(1) *What is the role of the spouse in preaching?* As more clergy couples go to seminary, an increasing number of spouses know more than the spouse doing the preaching. This is the case in my family. I spent many sermons interpreting my wife's facial expressions. On several occasions the look on my beloved's face made me quickly insert, "But there are other ways to look at this." As I get older, I find that one advantage of failing eyesight is no longer being able to distinguish between "slow down," "say something funny," and "don't go there."

(2) *How long should a sermon be?* The correct length for a sermon is 10 percent shorter than that of your predecessor. Preaching is an arena in which consumers want less for their money. People who applaud for encores and triple overtime will be irreparably twisted out of joint if worship lasts until 12:15. Churchgoers love to say things like "I never heard a bad ten-minute sermon" or "There are three steps to a good sermon—good introduction, good conclusion, keep them close together." These are, of course, painfully old jokes, but in general, "Quit while you're ahead" is better advice than "Keep going. You're on a roll."

(3) *What kind of pulpit Bible should I use?* The more evangelical your church, the heavier and darker the Bible needs to be. Only youth pastors have multicolored Bibles. Publishers are adding to their line of specialty Bibles (e.g., *The Jogger's Bible*, *The Stenographer's Bible*). *The Weary Minister's Bible* (available only in large print) will be a best-seller.

(4) *Eugene Lowry's* Homiletical Plot *is confusing and David Buttrick's* Homiletic: Moves and Structures *is complicated. Could you give me a simple, practical form for sermon outlines?* One helpful, easy to understand outline is this:

I. What I hope to say
II. What I think you are willing to hear
III. What James Forbes said about this
IV. What I wish I said

Three Insightful Homiletical Tips More than Worth the Price of this Book

(1) Be extremely careful with hand gestures.

(2) Don't use stupid, stifling, and sterilizing alliteration. It doesn't gladden, glorify, or glitter gracefully.

(3) Don't preach every Sunday. The old saw is, "If you're good you deserve the time off. If you're lousy they deserve it." The Sunday between Christmas and New Year's is, by canon law, a day on which the associate pastor is required to preach.

Stuff That Isn't in the Bible but Should Be

One of the great joys of ministry is discovering that life is a sermon illustration. If you are an educated clergyperson, you have already been advised to carry a notepad everywhere you go and write down everything that might be anything.

If Sunday's sermon is on grief, you should listen to country music. You can use "Write me a note to remind me to remember to forget about you," but be judicious with "Take this job and shove it."

Reference any television show you actually enjoy to illustrate the immorality of our culture. *Friends* and *The Sopranos* are excellent examples of shows with which to do this. Don't use soap operas as this indicates you are home during the day.

Share your struggles by telling stories of your humble beginnings in ministry, shoveling snow off the church steps with old Sunday school quarterlies.

Show that you're hip and modern with references to cell phones, Google, and Dave Matthews.

Read so you can tell them what you read. If you like Jürgen Moltmann, quote Jürgen Moltmann. If they end up thinking you're smart, so be it.

Quote Ralph Vaughn Williams and Robin Williams in the same sermon, Billy Graham and Billy Crystal, Eduard Schweizer and Eddie Murphy.

If your preaching is stale, have a baby. This is especially effective for female preachers. Ministers have children so that they will never run out of sermon illustrations. Live a funny life so you'll have more material.

Pulpit Envy

The key to joy in preaching is accepting that seminary trained us, more than anything else, to be sermon critics. We're so well-versed in what makes preaching good that we end up surprised when nobody stands in line to buy our sermon transcripts. Jealousy is an occupational hazard. Unless you're a preaching superstar like Fred Craddock or Barbara Brown Taylor (Fred, Barbara, if you're reading this, I am so thrilled), you don't sound like Fred Craddock or Barbara Brown Taylor. Don't you suspect that on some Sundays even Fred and Barbara don't sound like Fred and Barbara? Not many people in your congregation listen to your sermons and think, "that's lousy exegesis," or "what a piece of convoluted syntax that was."

We assume great preachers always plumb the depths of the text, but sometimes it's okay to stay on the surface. We've looked hard for a way to fit in a funny joke. Some Sundays we may be tempted to start with, "Today's sermon includes some stuff that wasn't good enough for last week's sermon."

Kathleen Norris said, "Preaching is like dropping a rose petal into the Grand Canyon and waiting for the echo." Maybe it's more like knocking over a brick wall with cheese puffs. The comments worshipers offer as they leave the sanctuary are unreliable echoes and cheese puff stains.

"I so enjoyed the sermon" (heard after a sermon on starvation in Africa).

"You really stepped on their toes today."

"I feel better when you finish your sermons."

"I never understood suffering until I heard you preach."

"Nice weather we're having."

Thank God for the blessed souls who come up with something appropriate to say ("Your sermon reminded me of something Thomas Merton said"), but don't think that's why you're preaching.

Every preacher has a different routine. My own begins with staring at the text, panning for gold, hunting for my church, my life, or God in the story. I write most of each sermon at the computer. In between periods of actually typing words, I wait for the life of my congregation or the grace of God to fill the open places.

Brett Younger

People drop by and apologize for interrupting my sermon preparation. It's hard to explain, and they might not want credit for the way it turns out, but we're all part of the joyful proclamation process. I am still overwhelmed by the sacredness of standing in a pulpit before a congregation filled with people who worship honestly and go beyond easy answers, pious platitudes, and worn clichés. They encourage preachers to tell the whole truth, both the light and the dark, the tears and the laughter.

Sunday Funnies

We know the panic of Friday afternoon without a word written, but we also know the joy of offering a true account of life. Like Edgar in King Lear, we can "speak what we feel, not what we ought to say." Make them laugh. Make them cry. Make them feel holy. Love the preparing, thinking, pondering, imagining, hoping, praying, and believing that something will happen. Nothing is better than getting to say, "This is what I believe God wants us to think about."

(four)

Sacred Puppetry

Every few days a religious catalog lands in the church mailbox pushing books on how to enliven worship. They promise "Worship That Will Turn Your Small Church into a Big Church" and "Worship That Will Turn Your Big Church into a Frighteningly Big Church." Many books offer ideas on punching up your preaching: "Fifty Funny Illustrations to Keep Them Laughing," "Sad, Sad, Sad Stories Guaranteed to Make Them Cry," "Safe, Simple, Shallow Sermons," "Booming, Busting Sermons for Baby Boomers and Baby Busters," and, for less articulate preachers, "Sermons You Can Mime."

Books on pepping up worship address other elements as well: "Silly Skits about Holy Truths," "Hymns You Can Whistle," "Children's Sermons to Make Adults Think You're Clever," and "Sacred Puppetry." Gospel gimmicks include rotating pulpits, bubbling baptisteries, and choir robes with plunging necklines.

It's no wonder that many pastors have given in to "worship lite." How much simpler would preaching be if we offered sermons with titles like "How to Have a Happy Marriage," "How to Have Happy Children," or "How to Have Happy Children Who Will Have Happy Marriages"?

What preacher hasn't wanted to shuck the tie or the high heels? Who's to say that clips from *Gladiator* don't illuminate the story of David and Goliath? What's wrong with Wild Cherry Pepsi and Pringles for the Lord's Supper?

What's wrong is that if pastors are expected to be entertainers, then most of us are Gary Coleman. If pastors are expected to be Dr. Phil, then we should have taken more than one pastoral care class. If pastors are expected to make everyone feel better, then we should admit to church members that a Grand Slam Breakfast and *The New York Times* is a better choice.

Real ministers know that joy isn't found in superficial happiness, but in digging deep until we find the real thing. We have to take the joy of worship seriously.

"V" Is for Visitor

Churches welcome guests in a variety of ways. Some pastors begin worship with: "I'd like all of our members to stand. Visitors should stay seated so that we can look down on you." Some congregations fill out visitor's cards at the beginning so that they can recognize guests from the pulpit at the end. This has led visiting parents to whisper to their children, "Put that card down, right now! I mean it!" Some churches try to get around this with, "If you are seated next to a visitor, raise his or her hand." Cards include name tags with ribbons that identify the wearer as "Guest," "Prospective Worker," or "Fresh Meat." We once visited a church where the minister told the congregation to tell ten people "God loves you and I do, too" and hug them. My wife was the only one to hug me. Lots of people hugged Carol.

Compulsory spontaneity may not be the way to go, but a friendly welcome is important. Ushers are technically responsible for greeting members and visitors. One usher in twenty speaks to strangers. Most ushers volunteer because they want to deal with power outages and fainting worshipers. They have no desire to speak to people, so the rest of us must pick up the slack.

The biggest obstacle is recognizing who is a visitor and who isn't. We've known the horror of asking, "Are you a visitor?" and hearing, "No, I'm a charter member." To which we should reply, "You should come more often."

It's usually safe to ask, "Have you been here before?" If they answer "yes" you can say, "I thought you looked familiar." If they say "no" you can respond, "I thought you looked unfamiliar."

Church members need to help one another in identifying visitors. A simple hand signal—perhaps a "V"—would work. We need to be careful when signaling, because visitors, like deer, are easily frightened. Sharing information is essential in offering a hospitable welcome. For example: "That's Sandra. She moved here from New York. Don't mention her accent."

Remembering visitors' names is extremely important. I use clever mnemonic devices. If a visitor's name is Victor Vincent I think "Victor, Vincent, and visitor all begin with V." If a guest's name is Brad Way, because I am at Broadway Baptist Church, I think "Brad Way is close to Broadway." If a visitor's name is Cal Berry, then hope your church's name is Calvary.

If you still don't remember a name, don't be embarrassed. Pretend that you do. Cleverly cover the fact that you don't know the person's name by referring to them as "our welcomed guest" until you remember it. When you introduce them you might say, "I know how to pronounce your name, but I like the way you say it." She will, of course, embarrass you by replying, "It's pronounced 'Cindy.'" I once asked, "How do you spell your first name?" It was J-a-c-k.

Gracious guests will appreciate almost anything, but there are a few things you shouldn't say:

"Why are you here?"

"You're sitting in the wrong pew."

"Are you a tither?"

"Would you like to sing with the choir?"

If you feel stuck, try one of these:

"I have just the Sunday school class for you. They have some real characters." (This works with every class.)

"A group of us go to lunch after church. Would you like to join us? We'll share our fries."

"Could I introduce you to Cal Berry?"

Visitors should act like visitors. Guests should arrive ten minutes before worship begins. (This will clearly mark them as visitors.) Proper guests act confused—as though the size of the building has bewildered them. Questions like "Where is the rest room?" clearly identify visitors. When someone says, "Hi, how are you?" thoughtful guests respond, "I'm fine. It's kind of you to ask, since I'm a visitor." Guests should say their name more than once as in: "Hi, I'm Marilyn. Most people call me Marilyn. You can call me Marilyn. Did I mention that I'm a visitor?"

If the members of your congregation still refuse to act in a welcoming manner, threaten them with mandatory hugging during the welcome time.

Signing In

My church is one of many that pass friendship registers as a way for members to welcome guests and learn each other's names. The process is simple. Those seated on the center aisle sign the register and pass it to the next person. The register moves to the end of the row, then back to the center so that each person sees each name. This system works well for church members, but is painfully redundant for the minister. How many times can you say, "Would those seated on the center aisle please sign the register and then pass it to the next person? The register should go to the end of the row, then back to the center so that each person sees each name," without your brain turning into leftover Wednesday night meatloaf?

In order to avoid beginning worship each Sunday by boring myself and others, I've encouraged worshipers to sign the friendship register in a variety of ways:

"Welcome to everyone who knows that they're a winner and to everyone who feels like a loser, to saints and to sinners and to all who are confused as to which they might be, to those who know that they're as sharp as a tack and to those who are wondering if in the pinball game of life their flippers are a little too far apart. Every one of you gets to sign the friendship register."

"Sign in because we're testing the theory that the smartest people sit closest to the front."

"Many people claim that Baptists (most denominations work here) are illiterate. Let's sign the worship register and prove them wrong."

"These days, when someone asks for your name, it is usually because they want it for telemarketing purposes. We are no exception. We can make money selling your name, so please sign the friendship register."

"Hezekiah 5:12 states: 'When thou enterest the temple of Lord thou shalt sign the holy book.'"

Sometimes the encouragement to sign the friendship register is tied to the seasons of the church year:

"Sign in and reserve your seat for Christmas Eve."

"You're not losing weight, you're not getting organized, and you're already behind on your reading, but you can keep your New Year's resolution to sign the friendship register each Sunday."

"Sign because there is a second blessing for those who come the Sunday after Easter."

"If your mother calls to see if you were in church on Mother's Day, we'll have a record."

I often point out the rewards of signing the register:

"If your friendship register has a star on it, present it to an usher after the service and see if he or she will give you a dollar."

"The row with the most signatures can come back next Sunday for free."

"If you sat on the wrong row by accident, this is a chance to learn some new names."

Other times it seems more appropriate to threaten people:

"If you sign in as a 'visitor,' you qualify to park in 'visitor's parking' by the front door. If you do not, you will be towed."

"Sign in, because God might not keep score, but we do."

"After you sign the register, please give us the names of the folks who don't so we can call and ask them what their problem is."

"The friendship register is not the Lamb's Book of Life—or is it?"

"Many Christian traditions believe in purgatory. If purgatory exists, no doubt there will be people there who spend extra time because they did not sign the friendship register. Even if you don't believe in purgatory, why take the chance?"

"If you don't sign the friendship register, we will start wearing name tags."

Does the Pastor Need a Haircut?

The attention church members pay to changes in worship gives naïve ministers the impression that everyone is concentrating on everything in worship. Such is not always the case. Some may be meditating on other matters.

Why are there eleven chimes at 10:50? The robe is fine, but that stole is garish. That was one lame friendship register joke. Who is that woman? What is her name? This hymn is pretty low church for us. If I had a sheave, I don't think I'd bring it in here. If I open my eyes during the prayer, will anyone notice? Why is the Scripture reading so long? Did she just read "thong"? I wonder if I could borrow a choir robe for Halloween? How many lights are in here? Could I throw a baseball into the baptistery? This hymn is why there are Catholic churches. How many tiles are on the ceiling? The sermon is never long enough. This preacher is magnificent. Couldn't they at least offer white wine as an option? What's for lunch?

Most people go to worship like Roger Ebert goes to the movies. They may find it interesting, but they can always name three ways it could be better.

Pastors go to school for an astonishing number of years to learn to guide worship. Musicians prepare extensively before leading hymns (which doesn't look that hard). We present the fruits of our hard labor to the congregation without offering enough suggestions on how it all works. Worshipers have the important tasks of praising, praying, listening, thanking, giving, and coming up with something kind to say when they shake the minister's hand. One form of worship education is to ask and answer the questions someone should ask but never does.

Asking Good Questions

How important is worship in the life of our church? Worship is the most crucial work of God's people. No higher service is possible than giving ourselves in worship. This is why every baby with a right-thinking parent is in the nursery not disturbing us.

Why do we read so much Scripture in worship? We are dependent on revelation because the biblical story sustains the church. The wind of the Spirit still blows through every verse of the sacred story. Listen to this randomly selected verse: "Esau is a hairy man, and I am a man of smooth skin" (Gen 27:11). Imagine how it would change our worship experience if we really meditated on this classic shaving text.

Why do we read responsively in worship? Hearing about our commitment is helpful, but speaking our commitment together requires commitment. This Sunday when I say, "The Lord be with you," the congregation will respond, "We promise to tithe."

Why don't people feel comfortable clapping in worship? The proper response to an expertly sung anthem is not accolades for the singers, but a prayer of thanksgiving to God. The ushers have been instructed to remove anyone who claps even once (and don't give me that "Clap your hands" stuff in the Psalms; we're not going to sacrifice goats either).

Why are our ushers so good-looking? Is this a requirement? This is a frequently asked question. The attractiveness of our ushers is a coincidence. Normal-looking people are welcome to serve as ushers.

Dry and Wet Sacraments

When we have a parent-child dedication (infant baptism without the water) at our church, we ask, "Do you promise in dependence on God's grace and with the help of the church to teach your child the gifts and claims of the Christian faith, and by prayer, word, and example to bring up your child in God's nurture, discipline, and instruction?" I am waiting for the right set of parents to ask, "Do you promise to make your child come to church as long as your child is under your roof? Do you promise to do everything in your power to convince this child that church is more fun than laser tag? Will you read the Bible out loud with as much excitement as you read the latest Harry Potter? Will you encourage your child to think of ministers as heroic?"

The first person I baptized was Keith. He was ten years old and I was nine years older. Keith and I talked about his baptism a dozen times. I went over it with Keith's parents. We discussed every imaginable possibility, or so I thought. Everyone somehow managed to forget to mention Keith's insane fear of water. I didn't find out about this fear until I saw it in his eyes as he stood at the edge of the baptistery. I led him down the steps slowly. I spoke the words of baptism, then I put my hand on his back and waited for him to lean back. I pulled on his shirt. He didn't move. He had no plans to move. I finally put my left hand on his shoulder to ever so gently push him under. He showed his first sign of life. He didn't want to be pushed ever so gently under. A small spot on the top of Keith's head never got wet. Churches that pride themselves on being 100 percent immersed would think Keith's baptism only 95 percent acceptable.

Most baptisms aren't nearly so exciting, only in part because most of us aren't afraid of water. We've toned baptism down. We shouldn't have brought baptisms inside. Most ministers baptize in a heated baptistery filled with tap water. They foolishly trust waders to keep them from getting wet. We ought to splash on the choir and drip in the sanctuary.

Baptisms ought to be outlandish. Once during a sermon on baptism I said, "In Ghana, Christian ministers sometimes walk down the aisle after a baptism and sprinkle water over the congregation to remind them that they were baptized." During the benediction I sprinkled water on a congregation of surprised but mostly smiling worshipers.

Missing *Sixty Minutes*

When I accepted my last two pastorates, it was because I felt the leadership of the Holy Spirit and because, unlike many Baptist churches, they have no Sunday evening worship.

Some people who want Sunday night worship have terrible reasons:

"Every time I watch *Sixty Minutes* I feel guilty. I imagine Mike Wallace asking why I'm not at church."

"When I think about my parents going to church every Sunday evening of their lives through an incredibly misplaced sense of obligation, I can't help but feel like I'm missing something."

"WWJDOSN? What would Jesus do on Sunday night?"

"I'll especially be glad to have something to do during the Super Bowl."

"Without Sunday night church, it's hard to tell who's really committed."

While imitating the church of the 1950s is seldom the best approach, an argument could nonetheless be made that additional services allow churches to explore their lack of creativity. Worshiping without the distraction of a crowd has advantages. More prospective soloists are available, because evening service standards are lower. Evening services give the pastor the opportunity to preach without a manuscript, notes, preparation, or, on occasion, any real idea of where she or he is going. Preaching through favorite books of the Bible (Leviticus, 2 Thessalonians) is a way to share half-baked (or completely uncooked) ideas.

Churches plan special events for evening services. On favorite hymn night, attenders have the opportunity to make people sing hymns that only they like.

Having another worship service means moving beyond the Christian calendar to celebrate government holidays. Who doesn't love Labor Day, Arbor Day, and Boxing Day services? Churches honor civic organizations at evening services—Boy Scouts, Rotarians, Freemasons, and Teamsters.

Bible drills and trivia quizzes offer those who grew up with Bible drills and trivia quizzes a chance to show off. Deacons, the worship committee, or nursery workers can lead worship.

My advice is still to run like a whirlwind from any suggestion to add services, but for those unfortunate souls whose schedules include evening worship, here are some wonderfully helpful ideas: pie night; preschoolers' musicales; blessing of the animals; using sermons someone else wrote ("God, even as you blessed this sermon when Martin Luther King Jr. preached it, bless it again"); inviting other ministers who don't have evening services (sharing the pain) to preach; field trips to other churches; Gideon speakers; dancers (not a good idea in some churches; use your own judgment); go-home-to-your-family night.

Name That Tune

Nothing is more inspiring and divisive in worship today than music. The wise minister gives up on making everyone happy. Making the minister happy is now, more than ever, the reasonable goal.

Contemporary worship music is beyond the understanding of some of us. I don't appreciate the subtle difference between an accompaniment tape and karaoke. I cannot sing "Praise the Lord, Oh Baby" with a straight face. I do like it when in an attempt to avoid empty ritual, women sing the first verse, men the second, and everyone stands on the third and closes their eyes on the fourth.

Most hymnbooks include two types of sacred hymns—those that can be sung and those that cannot. Ministers find joy in making worshipers sing words they do not mean. What BMW-driving business executive means "Take my silver and my gold"? It's not within a million miles of the truth, but if you make them sing it, then someday, after years of humming at a subconscious level, they may give money away without knowing it was your fault.

Choosing music is different for each congregation. Evangelical churches lean to country music, formal churches to classical, and charismatic churches to rock and roll. In some churches, ministers know that they can include a drummer because people in their church love drums. In other churches, ministers can bring in a drummer when a particular piece of music calls for it. In churches like mine, drums are appropriate when Hell freezes over (or the drums are part of a full percussion section in a sixty-piece orchestra).

Picking the Songbook

Choosing a new hymnal is a perilous opportunity that is seldom touched on in seminary classrooms. At some point, if you encourage the youth to drop the old hymnals from the balcony, you may get to pick a hymnal you like. (If you are in a church where a denominational hierarchy hands down a particular hymnbook without any input on your part, then pretend you are glad and skip this part. Reading this section will only make you jealous.)

Ministers who did not experience this decision as a gift tell horror stories about their church's attempts to choose a new hymnal. Congregations end up singing out of wildly unpopular hymnals held together with Elmer's glue, Scotch tape, and rubber bands because they can't agree on a new one. Charter members leave because they are on the losing side of the "Should the new hymnal be sky blue or navy blue?" vote. Former ministers of music work as convenience store clerks because they chose a hymnal without "Amazing Grace" in it.

We need to give lip service to conflicting values that warrant our appreciation and understanding: the balance of tradition and contemporaneity, the allergies some people have toward some types of hymns, and the absolute goofiness people exhibit when choosing a new hymnal. Any hymnal with nothing offensive to anyone will fit on a three-by-five card.

Here is a good process to follow in choosing a new hymnal: Choose a hymnal selection committee that has no more than one crazy person (harder than usual as you are dealing with musicians). Choose a chair with no knowledge of music but great love for the pastor. Lead the committee in working hard to receive and take seriously the congregational input with which you agree. Prepare a survey with questions like these: Do you like singing new hymns or are you completely stagnant musically and as a human being? Would you pay for a hymnal? Why not?

Keep saying things like "I trust that we will be open to God, discerning our best sense of what will support God's movement among and through us, and seek to sing together in the spirit of Christ" even as you keep your back to the wall.

Ye Who are Weary Come Home

Some people assume that a real worship service hasn't taken place unless it ends with a constantly interrupted invitation hymn. After a long sermon, a preacher with a booming voice says something along the lines of "This is the time of commitment. If you feel God pulling at your heart, then you need to come forward. If you feel something in your heart and you're not sure what it is, you need to come. No matter what you're feeling, you need to come, as we stand and sing."

Time is now fleeting, the moments are passing, passing from you and from me.

"If you would like to rededicate your life, this is the time for that decision. You may have rededicated your life fifty times; come again. Maybe you rededicated your life last night, but had a bad day today. Come again, as the choir hums."

Oooooooooooooooooohh. "If you are a male, then you may be called to full-time Christian service, or if you are really brave then you should be a missionary. Come as the pianist plays only the black keys."

Shadows are gathering, deathbeds are coming, coming for you and for me.

"I know many of you wish this invitation were over. Maybe your legs have fallen asleep from standing so long. Even so, I think that there is someone here who needs to come forward." (A husband whispers to his wife, "Do you think you could rededicate your life? I'm missing the kickoff.") "Let's have every head bowed and every eye closed." (More than two-thirds of the eyes are closed.) "If you are a member of the church, pray for those who are not. If you are not a member, then know that there are people sitting near you who are telekinetically pushing you to the front. Raise your hand if you feel like you need to make a decision. Raise your hand if someday you might make some decision. Raise your hand if you want to encourage me. If no one comes on this verse, then we'll close the invitation." The less spiritual members of the congregation offer a sigh of relief.

"Walking the aisle" has its roots in the 1830s when Charles Finney began utilizing the "anxious bench" where those in need of salvation were to sit. The job of those who had already made decisions was to stare the anxious into the kingdom. This practice evolved into the bizarre evangelical custom of shaking the preacher's hand as the primary expression of the desire to become a Christian. Most churches that ask people to walk the aisle will keep doing so, but they need to know how peculiar it is.

Quown Him

It hasn't been a good week to be a minister. You had a long, depressing deacons' meeting (the issue was the color of the new offering envelopes), lost your VISA card, and argued with your daughter over piercing a body part that you didn't know could be pierced. On Saturday night, you try to go to sleep to the barking of the neighbor's German shepherd. You wake up late to discover that the alarm didn't go off (you set the time but neglected to turn it on). You rush to church and hurry through half of your normal preparations. You fall into your chair just before the organist begins the opening hymn. "Crown him with many crowns, the lamb upon his throne. Hark! How the heavenly anthem drowns all music but its own." Slowly but surely, your thoughts move beyond your own crises and problems. "Awake my soul, and sing of him who died for me." The music gets past your lips and penetrates your heart. As you give thanks for God's goodness, you sense that there is more than just this congregation singing. "Thy praise and glory shall not fail throughout eternity." For thousands of years, ministers have been going to worship even when they don't feel like it. For most of the church's history, ministers haven't had deacons' meetings, offering envelopes, VISA cards to lose, or teenage daughters, but ministers have long been singing when they don't sleep well and are running late. After what I perceived as poorly received sermons, I used to quietly sing the closing hymn like Elmer Fudd, as in, "Quown him wif many quowns, de wamb upon his fwown." It was a way of humoring myself. I don't do that nearly so often anymore. Instead, I try to recognize that in the act of worship, even when we're leading and it wasn't all that we hoped for, we can remember the joy that made us want to be ministers in the first place.

five

The Lord Be with You, but I'm in a Meeting

If asked how the church began, some people picture a group of old, white men in dark suits gathered around a long oak table. Peter turns the page on a flip chart and says, "I've listed what I think are the keys to an effective organization:

(1) Dynamic small groups.
(2) Dynamic programs.
(3) Dynamic financial resources.
(4) Dynamic parking and facilities.

Keep these four in mind as we hear the reports from the committees on procedures and job descriptions."

Ministers sign on to help a group of disciples become a community of grace, study Holy Scripture in the original languages, proclaim release to the captives and sight to the blind, and visit widows and orphans in their affliction, but by the second day you figure out that you are the mayor of Administration City. Administer comes from a Greek word meaning "to minister" or, according to one ancient interpretation, "a big pain." One suspect clergy in ten enlists because he or she wants to be in charge of committee meetings, promotion, budgets, and buildings.

At seminary, everyone's least favorite course (including the professor's) was Church Leadership. The textbooks, which you find on the "Free Books" table at used bookstores, were breathtakingly dull: *Management of Organizational Behavior: Utilizing Human Resources* (not as much fun as the title leads you to believe); *The Management of Ministry: Leadership, Purpose, Structure, and Community* (don't wait for the movie); and *Twelve Keys to an Effective Church* (number 10: adequate landscaping). We wrote papers like "Long-Range Planning Committees: What Is God Thinking?" We role-played deacons' meetings ("We have to do a better job of managing organizational behavior and utilizing our human resources." "But it's vitally important that we address leadership, purpose, structure, and community! And adequate landscaping!").

You might expect seminaries to spend time teaching students how to do the things they will be expected to do every day, but most professors find Greek and Hebrew more interesting. Seminaries should teach mail merging and e-mail (knowing the difference between "reply" and "reply all" would have been extremely beneficial to me at one moment in my ministry).

No matter how fine our training, nothing completely prepares us for the wide range of the minister's administrative duties. The church leadership section of Christian book catalogs (tomorrow's "Free Books") keeps getting bigger. Some titles make it sound like the church is in bad shape: *From Stuck to Unstuck: Overcoming Congregational Impasse*; *The Trouble with the Church*; *God's Frozen People*, and—how's this for a catchy title—*The Enemy in the Pew*. One expert on church administration knows the target audience—*Never Call Them Jerks: Healthy Responses to Difficult Behavior*.

Fantasy-based Planning

For some of us, the phrases "church administration," "committee meetings," and "church planning" elicit the same weeping and gnashing of teeth as the phrase "root canal." Long-range planning committees have for years identified purposes, stated objectives, and determined goals. The mission of traditional long-range planning was to have long, excruciatingly dull committee meetings that produce long, excruciatingly dull spiral-bound reports filled with dates, dollar amounts, and ideas like (1) increase Sunday morning attendance by 18 percent, (2) remodel the children's building with a *Veggie Tales* theme, and (3) purchase reversible choir robes with Velcro stoles. These reports were put on the shelf with *Everybody Sing-n-Celebrate!*, *The Georgia Presbyterian Annual 1981*, and the last long-range planning committee report.

An increasingly popular form of long-range church planning is market-driven planning. This form carefully studies the competition. In many cities in the Deep South, the "competition" has traditionally been understood to be the Methodists or the Baptists. After scouting the opposition, the church looks for a niche among people groups. Where do left-handed people go to worship? Is there a church reaching out to dentists? Can we be the church for displaced Luxembourgers?

A third form of planning is known as reality-based planning (as opposed to fantasy-based planning). When planners utilize this system, they work for incremental changes: increase the Sunday morning attendance by 1.8 percent, paint the three-year-olds' room avocado green, begin a fund for Velcro stoles, and write a note to Dr. Freud—the new left-handed dentist from Luxembourg.

Multiple-scenario planning lays out a series of possibilities and forms a contingency plan for each. What will we do if our Sunday morning attendance suddenly increases 18 percent? What if someone leaves lots of money for remodeling, but we want reversible choir robes? What if Dr. Freud comes and brings other dentists with him?

Visionary leader planning is one person announcing, "I have been to the mountaintop. Follow me." This approach is particularly unpopular with ministers who have raced halfway up Everest only to turn and see that no one else has broken camp. The opposite approach doesn't work any better. Ministers with their ears to the ground get run over.

In our meetings and committees, rather than debate the merits of copy machine contracts, we can stop the conversation—at least for a moment—by asking, "How can we act more like Jesus?"

Killing Time

Charles Dickens was at a church meeting when he said, "I have a suggestion. Why don't we move to a table, sit around the table holding hands, and see if we can make contact with the living?"

Committees have a bad reputation, but meetings can be wonderfully rewarding if you follow a few simple rules:

- Figure out which committees are just glad to get together and enjoy getting together with them.
- Figure out which committees enjoy thinking deep thoughts and enjoy thinking deep thoughts with them.
- Figure out which committees enjoy sarcastic comments and enjoy trading sarcastic comments with them.
- Figure out which committees work and be thankful for them.
- When you recommend committee members, choose people who are unreservedly enthusiastic about you.
- When you suggest members for the finance committee, nominate people who are paid more than you. (No one will vote for you to make more money than they make.)
- Bring donuts.

Church Secretaries Rule

You don't learn who is in charge by looking at the names on the back of the order of worship. In most church hierarchies, the secretary is only a little lower than the angels. The unfortunate pastors who do not understand the secretary's importance end up copying resumes at Kinko's. The pastor who does not get along with the secretary has no life of which to speak.

Here's a brief test to determine if you have a good secretary:

(1) A salesperson from "Gospel Glory Gadgets" calls. The secretary says,
   a. "Let me let you talk to the pastor."
   b. "I'll take down the information. He'll call you. He may not be able to get back with you until after the Second Coming."

(2) The Director of Missions drops by to see if the pastor will serve on the Associational Long-range Planning Committee. The secretary says,
   a. "I'm sure he would enjoy that."
   b. "He's too busy right now doing God's work."

(3) The pastor takes his son to an afternoon track meet. When someone asks for him, the secretary says,
   a. "He's at the race track."
   b. "He's not here right now. He must be praying."

Anyone who answers "a" to any of these questions should set his or her sights on a lesser career.

According to official job descriptions, "The Administrative Secretary is responsible to the pastor and other ministers for performing duties as assigned by them, and for the secretarial duties related to the pastoral, educational, and financial dimensions of the church. These duties include, but are not limited to, the following . . . ." Forty-three specific tasks are listed, including "answering the phone and the mail; preparing newsletters and orders of worship; overseeing everything that has anything to do with the building." The forty-three don't include dispensing lots of information (when the phone company started charging for information, some churches added a second secretary to give out phone numbers), deciphering the pastor's handwriting, returning everything that's lost, trusting everybody and counting the cards, and remembering what should be remembered and forgetting what should be forgotten.

Good secretaries go beyond what's required. One of the secretary's primary responsibilities is protecting the pastor with helpful comments like:

"That's not a visitor. That's a deacon."

"Don't refer to your IBM as a parsonal computer. It's not funny."

"In your newsletter article you may want to include the phrase 'There may be other interpretations.'"

Do not be offended when people come to the office and say, "I was looking for the secretary. I don't think you can help me."

The Gospel Message

One of your first administrative duties may be to put your voice on the church's answering machine. Most churches have a message like this: "You have reached the church office. Our office hours are 8:30-5:00 Monday through Friday. Christian education classes are each Sunday at 9:30. Worship is at 11:00. If you'd like to leave a message, please do so after the tone." The message is so well-written, crisply delivered, and uplifting that the monumental step of changing the message leads to serious soul-searching. What bigger question is there than "What message does our community of grace most need to share?"

Answering machines should reflect the theological distinctives of particular churches. For instance:

Liturgical churches—"The Lord be with you, but we're out right now."

Calvinist churches—"We're not in the office, but God knew you were going to call."

Charismatic churches—"Hallelujah! Hallelujah! Hallelujah! Leave a hallelujah when you hear the tone (we can always use another)."

Evangelical churches—"We're not in, but we don't want to miss this opportunity to ask, 'Have you heard of the four spiritual laws?'"

Quaker churches—"We're not in right now, but you don't need us. The Light is within you."

Baptist churches—"We can't agree on what to say on this answering machine, but we strongly believe in your right to leave the message you feel led to leave."

You can put messages on your machine that promote particular church programs:

"If it's Wednesday, then we're making dinner. You can't beat the food or the price."

"Each Sunday morning, Christian education classes begin at 10:00 for the young adults and at 9:30 for everyone else."

"This is the choir director. When you leave your message, open your mouth, breathe deeply, and enunciate."

Put a special message on the machine during stewardship emphases: "We're not in right now, but if you would like to leave a message you may do so. If you're calling about a financial contribution, call us at home."

The answering machine message is a big deal, so ask church members to leave their ideas for it on the answering machine. You may end up with something simple: "We're sorry we missed your call. We're probably praying. We're very spiritual."

You've Got Mail

Some of the best mail in the world comes addressed to "Pastor." (This rule does not extend to e-mail. Never have so many with so little to say had such an opportunity to say it. The contemporary version of the Lord's Prayer includes "Deliver us from e-mail." The good, free stuff always comes through the US Postal Service.) I receive inspirational pocket pals, bookmarks with inspirational praying hands, and inspirational calendars with the words "Compliments of Your Church" printed on them—available for 79 cents each.

License tag frames can be used for advertising and fundraising. If you order 250 "We attend *Insert Your Church Name Here*" tags, they are only 99 cents each. Ministers get free ink pens. I have received nifty pens with crosses on them that say "Compliments of Brett Younger." When people are trying to decide what they most need in a community of faith, many say, "I'm looking for a church where the ministers give away pens with their names on them."

My all-time favorite free gift is the church donut/carry-all box that includes a place for your church business card and a list of ways to extend your donut box ministry. The manufacturers encourage ministers to "imagine all the things you can carry in these church donut/carry-all boxes" (donuts, donut holes, éclairs). If you are wondering, "Is the box FDA approved?" wonder no more; it is! The instructions suggest you use these in prison ministry or "marriage encounters"—I can't guess what that means. One hundred of these babies cost only $199 plus $17.87 shipping per case. If you're part of a church that wouldn't immediately order a case, be grateful.

Brett Younger

God's Funny Books

Not since Bibles began rolling off Gutenberg's press has one publication been so consistently anticipated. Church pictorial directories are God's funny books. What's more fun than looking at a church directory, knowing that in ten years you'll realize how goofy you looked?

Church directories are wonderful even though there are limitations. The people in your directory don't look like the people in your church. Eight-year-old boys (and a few thirty-year-old boys) wear ties that make them look less like themselves than anyone else.

At times, directories make churches look sterile, well dressed, and like every other church. The candid action shots aren't candid enough. Would it be more realistic to picture a nursery worker smiling at contented babies or changing a diaper?

The division of photographs into family units is ecclesiologically debatable. The church is, after all, made up of the people who recognize that we're all one family. Church directories have pictures of groups that are good families—Sunday school classes, prayer groups, bowling teams—but they don't include funny captions: "Has the kitchen crew gotten into the cooking sherry again?" The most church-like picture might be one life-sized photograph of everyone in your flock, but Olan Mills won't go for it.

Encourage your congregation to treat your church directory like a high school annual. Do you remember parties where everyone signed each other's annuals? "Love ya," "Good luck always," "I hope you always stay just the way you are now." (What kind of curse was that?) Sometimes the comments were theological:

"If in heaven we don't meet,
if we start to get the heat,
if it ever gets too hot,
RC Cola hits the spot."

Imagine filling each other's church directories with heartfelt sentiments:

"Reagan, if you hadn't been on the finance committee, it wouldn't have been nearly so much fun!"

"Charlotte, we had some good times in the women's Bible study. Thanks for the muffins!"

"Lauren, I loved being your roomie at youth camp. Save me the top bunk!"

"Rufus, I'm so glad we were in Adult 5 together. We need someone sane in there!"

"Betty, thanks for your work on the kitchen committee. I think of you every time I microwave!"

"Annette, I can't believe you're rotating off the diaconate next year. It won't be the same without you!"

"Hazel, I'm so happy you're in old man Bellinger's class. You make it wacky!"

Joyful ministers are not afraid to say, "U R 2 sweet 2 B 4-got-10."

Wall Street and West Wing

The most helpful suggestion for church administrators may be to recognize whom you are supposed to guide.

Calvin Curry is the first to arrive. He's been a deacon for forty years and has been the first one there at 95 percent of the meetings. Calvin serves on the finance committee and teaches a men's Bible study. He has lots of insurance and blames the Beatles for much of the evil in the world. He's a clean-shaven World War II veteran who thinks there's been nothing good on television since *Hogan's Heroes*. Calvin is Brooks Brothers, Ford Explorer, the Dallas Cowboys, steak and potatoes, *Wall Street Week*, classical music, *The Washington Post*, and John Wayne.

Marc McAlister shows up five minutes late—early for Marc. He's been a deacon for a year and has yet to show up on time or figure out how he got to be a deacon. Marc serves on the hunger awareness committee and volunteers at the local food bank. He owns almost everything in the Land's End catalog and blames Ronald Reagan for much of the evil in the world. He's disappointed that he was too young to officially dodge the Vietnam draft and thinks there's been nothing good on television since *M*A*S*H*. Marc is Birkenstocks, Volkswagen, the Oakland Raiders, cappuccino, *West Wing*, classic rock, *Mother Earth News*, and Michael Moore. Marc and Calvin are amazed that they go to the same church.

The treasurer gives her report: "I have checked and rechecked the numbers. At first I assumed there must be a mistake, but no matter how many times I go over it, it comes out the same. I can't believe I'm saying this, but last year our income was significantly more than our expenditures. What should we do?"

Marc is the first to respond. "I think it would be wrong for us to keep even a dime of this money. I vote we give it all away to other ministries."

Calvin replies thoughtfully, "I understand how you feel, Marc" (even though he's sure he doesn't), "but I think it would be wrong for us not to care for our church. There are maintenance issues that we've ignored for too long. My young friend should see this as an opportunity for us to strengthen the base from which we do ministry."

Marc says kindly, "I understand what you're saying Calvin" (even though he's sure he doesn't), "but if we don't give this money away, then, my dear old acquaintance, we've missed an opportunity to support ministries that serve people we don't get to help."

Calvin's face is turning pink when he says, "Marc, if we want to do something for those ministries that will matter ten years from now, when your hair is a reasonable length, we'll make sure there's a strong church here to keep supporting them."

Marc's face is red when he says:, "Cal, back when you had hair, surely you wondered who would want to go to a church that doesn't realize that there are people who need our help."

Crimson Calvin answers, "Son, you must realize that we wouldn't have money to give away if people had not been looking after this church since before you broke your first law. This church wouldn't be here without people caring for it."

Marc, now maroon, adds, "If this church only had members who think it's 1959, then we would forget that we're here to care for people who need our help now."

A good pastor will be the first one in the room to realize that Marc and Calvin both have a point. Helping Calvin remember what it's like to be young and idealistic and helping Marc recognize the amazing commitment it takes to care for the same congregation for an entire lifetime is a joy. The church needs priests and prophets, Matthew the tax collector and Simon the Zealot, ties and tie-dyes, maintenance and mission, cathedrals and soup kitchens, deacons and church administrators.

six

Eccentric Evangelism, Edifying Education, Mesmerizing Ministry, and Pain-relieving Pastoral Care

Reaching out, growing up, getting to work, and feeling better make up the actual but unwritten job description of a joyful minister. Evangelism, education, ministry, and pastoral care are tasks that are older than we are, and yet the work must always be brand new. Figuring out what this means in your ministry is half the battle.

I grew up in congregations that tried every evangelism program that came down the pike. We were the church with the sign out front: "Be ye fishers of men. You catch 'em. God'll clean 'em."

I am a veteran of all kinds of evangelistic acronyms: the WIN program—Witness Involvement Now; EE—Evangelism Explosion; ACTION—I can't remember what all the letters stand for, but I'm relatively certain C was for Christian. I knocked on doors and harassed strangers on the street. I could recite the Roman Road and Four Spiritual Laws in my sleep. Now I shudder when I think of the blows

I struck to the gospel. I shake both when I see the fresh blows of evangelism reduced to salesmanship and when I see those sitting the whole thing out in reaction to that.

You're sitting in a meeting where the chair of the evangelism committee begins his report: "Our Monday night visitation program has slowed a bit. The numbers aren't as big as I wish. Some of you know that Second Church says that they have more people in Sunday school than we have, though I suspect they are counting members who are sleeping in, pregnant women twice, and any fly that flits through the building. Anyway, this Saturday we are going to start a new program that the convention has just come out with. The program is called "You Sinners Better Lock Your Door." At 9:00 on Saturday morning, we'll have a thirty-minute training session to memorize our lines. This should be easy for those of you who memorized the verses for "You Sinners Better Pretend You're Not Home." This program will be a little different because you will receive extra credit for married thirty- to thirty-five-year-olds as well as the usual bonus points for millionaires and tithers. We'll wear these attractive gold S lapel pins. When people ask, 'Why are you wearing an S?' we'll answer, 'We're Super Christians. Would you like to be a Super Christian, too?' We'll go to every house in our part of town and leave these slightly offensive tracts for people who aren't home. Denominational headquarters estimates that for every 111 houses we visit, we will find a prospect. Are there any questions?"

The last hand the chair of the evangelism committee wants to see is the only hand in the air: "I would like to point out to the earnest if overzealous chair of the evangelism committee that if we knock on 111 doors and find one prospect, then 110 people may have decided they don't want anything to do with a bunch of nuts with gold S's on their lapels. I won't be wearing your costume jewelry. I refuse to let you make me feel like a door-to-door encyclopedia salesman and, by the way, I would like for someone on your committee to scrape the 'I found it' bumper sticker off my car. I won't learn your canned presentation, because I don't think I have any business telling a total stranger that her life is wrong because she doesn't believe exactly what I believe. God may be happier with her than with me. I don't think we as a church should have anything to do with self-interested institutional spiels, church growth gimmicks, or techniques usually associated with the sale of used cars. Most people don't want to be bothered and I don't want to bother them. I want to belong to a church that has the good sense to leave me and everyone else alone. I want the kind of church that you don't notice unless you're looking for it."

The chair of the evangelism committee is silent for just a moment. "I would like to respond by pointing out that the people who criticize our evangelism programs don't do squat. They do nothing, naught, nada, zilch, zip, zero. If you are ever willing to do anything more than warm a pew three Sundays a month, please let us know what that might be. In the meantime, consider the possibility that there might be some people out there who are tired of being alone, and quit complaining about people who are willing to speak to them."

The battle lines are drawn between "let's try another program" and "we're in the phone book if they want to call." At this moment someone turns to you and says, "Pastor, what do you think?"

The pastor's joyful calling is to show the people in our church a better way. Evangelism, at its best, is listening to others talk about what's most important in their lives and then sharing what's most important in our lives. We shouldn't wait for the bank that holds the mortgage to encourage us to be more evangelistic, because, if we can get past both the acronyms and the perils of introversion, it's BF—Big Fun.

Holy Heretics

The church is almost 2,000 years old and Sunday school is 200 at the most, but sometimes it seems like it's the other way around. As

I remember it, before Mrs. Butler began the prelude, Alton Weatherby would give the Sunday school report:

> We had eighty-four today—two more than last Sunday, but three less than a year ago. Seventy-eight brought their Bibles, eleven read their Bible every day, six studied their lesson, and eighty-two of the eighty-four were on time. I'm sorry about that. Mrs. Weatherby is cooking a roast and apparently I wasn't much help. The Dorcas class was the biggest with twelve. Six of those were here for the Peach family reunion, but they couldn't stay for preaching. The Ruth class had all seven of its members present for the ninth week in a row. The streak should continue until Mrs. Vivian's bursitis acts up again. The Friendship class had 100 percent lessons studied. Congratulations to both of them. Remember that next week is Great Day in the Morning High Attendance Day. I hope you all come to Sunday school next Sunday.

Most churches don't have Sunday school reports anymore, but if we did, they might sound something like this:

> Jorene Swift, twelve days old, was at Sunday School for the second time. Miss Pattie thinks Jorene likes it though she hasn't said anything. Harrison and Maya made a church out of blocks in Mrs. Hazel's class. Like many who grow up in church, they had moments when they were tempted to kick the church in.
>
> After careful consideration, Sherry Ledbetter's first and second graders have decided to change the name of the fifth book of the Bible to "Deunatronomy" because it sounds better. David Mallette showed rare insight when he asked if Hercules was one of the patriarchs. Charlotte Carpenter has been teaching the third and fourth graders the Lord's Prayer, Beatitudes, and Great Commission. If there's time at the end of the year, Charlotte will make them memorize the Hebrew alphabet and selected passages from the Mishnah. Amy Cooper noticed that the boys and girls in the fifth and sixth grade class are sitting about a foot closer to one another than they did at the beginning of the year.

Fran Patterson led the middle schoolers in a discussion of wisdom. Libby Patterson would have smiled if she had heard Mary Patterson say, "It's what your grandmother says."

Tom Roberts has been working hard with the senior high. None of them fall for it anymore when he tells them to turn to Hezekiah.

The Singles' class has been reading Anne Lamott's *Traveling Mercies*. Jason McCoy wondered aloud if Anne is dating anyone seriously. The young marrieds have been working through Genesis. Princeton Williams asked, "If you were Sarai, how would you react to Abram's announcement that he's rented a U-Haul?" Cindy and Roland Johnson's Married with Young Children's class has been studying the pastor's sermon text. They have stopped predicting what the preacher will say and now go straight to what the preacher should say.

The Holy Heretics have been discussing Marcus Borg's *Meeting Jesus Again for the First Time*. David Grebel said, "Listening to the story may be more important than deciding the answers," and no one disagreed.

Harold Dill's class is studying the Book of Mark at the rate of four verses a week—or about 1/100th of the speed with which Mark wrote it.

The Ruth class is glad to be through with five lessons on apocalyptic literature. Iona Richardson thinks that if she doesn't hear the word "apocalyptic" again until the end of the world, it will be too soon.

The cantankerous old men's class covered predestination, homosexuality, and genetics and still had time for a second cup of coffee. They love to disagree, because after forty years together they are family.

Whenever I'm tempted to think of the weekly hour of Christian education as one more part of the routine, I try to look more closely. In every class there are moments when the gentle wind of the Spirit blows for anyone paying attention.

Is That You, Jimmy Carter?

With increasing frequency, ministers are expected to do manual labor as a way of sharing ministry with their parishioners. Ministry outside one's comfort zone can feel like an interruption. You may feel like you should be back at the church writing a newsletter column, but humility is a lesson learned in more ways than one.

Volunteering that requires a "waiver of liability" is almost never a good sign. The form contains the ominous declaration that "as a volunteer, you are not covered by Workers Compensation Insurance." It does not say, "chances are good that you, with your laughable lack of skills, will be disfigured beyond recognition," but it could.

I spend every moment with Habitat for Humanity pretending to be adequate. At my last such attempt, the project manager encouraged me: "We have paint, caulk, and trim. We can cover up everything you do." My goal is to be assigned work no one actually needs to do. (One minister friend was strangely offended when given the job of painting pre-painted trim.) I live in fear of hearing, "Put a nail in that real quick."

When I listen carefully, what I hear is more interesting than fear-provoking:

"Aren't the little curly-cues that the saw makes cute?"

"You might want to count again."

"Is your phone ringing? If it's not, I should stop hammering for a while."

"Aren't you just Jimmy Carter?"

"Are you sure we're building camaraderie?"

On my last trip to the construction site, I started out with a hammer, but someone took it away. Another person handed me an X-acto knife, but I knew that was a bad idea. For a while I tried to make a job out of picking up things that real workers had dropped—nails, pencils, spare change. I tried to look like I knew what I was doing. I hung a nail out of my mouth for a while, but everybody knew the truth. When I heard a serious carpenter talking about "deadwood," I thought he was referring to me. I was finally asked to work on an important job with a Methodist pastor. Sara and I were to put up the Tyvek weatherization wrap. It's gift-wrapping a house with a staple gun. We moved quickly but carefully. Each time we finished a wall one of us would say, "That's a wrap," and laugh. Even at my level of expertise, it didn't take long, so I ended up admiring my work and talking to the project director. The house we were working on was advertised as a clergy-built house, which makes everything about the house suspect. Most of the workers had tools that made them look like they weren't pastors—tool belts, levels, measuring tape, and hammers that looked used. I asked the director how many of the people working on the house were ministers. She was defensive. "Some of them. The really inept clergy put the Tyvek wrap around the house."

Working with Habitat is embarrassing and amazing. I keep waiting for profound, spiritual thoughts to flood my consciousness. The penetrating insights never come, but I have learned a lot while working with the organization. Sheetrock is neither a sheet nor rock. Clockwise to tighten; counterclockwise to start all over. Measure twice, cut once. Habitat T-shirts and bumper stickers make ministers look socially aware even when we're socially unconscious. The only thing worse than hitting your thumb with a hammer is hitting half your thumb. It's foolish to put on coconut-scented sun block if you're working inside a house. People will make fun of you. The way in which I am least likely to be like Jesus is by becoming a carpenter.

It's remarkable that thousands of people—skilled and ministerial—pound nails, cut the ends off rafters, paint, pick up pencils, and gift wrap. The best things ministers do can feel like interruptions. At the time I spend too much energy thinking I should be doing something else—"I should be writing something inspiring." Ministers need to stop dwelling on when they will get to the next task long enough to recognize that what may first feel like an interruption is actually a joyful part of our job.

Free Popsicles

Like Habitat houses, hospitals are a surprising source of joy. Some ministers feel uncomfortable visiting hospitals. They don't enjoy labyrinthine corridors, ICU Gestapo guards, and reminders of their own mortality. A disproportionately large number of people there aren't feeling their best. Some pastors go to the hospital only when they're stuck on the sermon. Here are suggestions to keep you from missing the joys of hospital visitation.

Be there. Pastors get points for showing up and lose points for not showing up. For this reason, it's often more fun to visit someone who doesn't expect you to show up.

Enter carefully. Don't forget to knock on the door before entering the room (a mistake ministers make only once).

Relax. People who worry that they will say the wrong thing end up saying almost nothing. If the patient asks, "Do you need some painkiller?" then he or she may have sensed that you are tense. A cheerful voice, caring heart, and listening ear go a long way, but there are a few inappropriate comments you should avoid:

"Did you hear that this hospital is going to be on *60 Minutes*?"

"That's the biggest needle I've ever seen."

"Could I get one of those free popsicles?"

"My late uncle had the same thing."

"Have you signed your organ donor card?"

Get out. If a doctor puts on a latex glove, it's time to go. If you hear yourself saying, "That's nothing. Let me tell you about my operation," then you're out of things to say. Hospital patients can tire easily. If the person you are visiting falls asleep, you should leave.

Don't be afraid to smile. Because hospitals are solemn places, some are apprehensive about laughing, but most of us have visited hospital rooms where we laughed as well as prayed. On some of those occasions, the laughter seems as holy as the prayers.

I Never Met Tim LaHaye

I arrived at the airport in time to catch an earlier flight, but I was the last one to get on the plane. Everyone was belted in and ready to go, so they glared like they had been waiting for me. I made my way to the back and located my assigned seat next to the window by a man who was pretending to be asleep.

"Excuse me, that's my seat."

"Oh, no, are you sure?"

The person on the row behind him exulted with frightening friendliness, "Come sit with me!"

The first rule of air travel is never to sit with a stranger who wants to sit with you. My new friend's name is Mondo—an Air Force mechanic and shortstop going to Atlanta for a weeklong softball tournament. Mondo's Air Force softball team was on the plane. I commented that I was glad my tax dollar was at work. Mondo momentarily stopped smiling. His shaved head is usually covered by a new baseball cap that he has just gotten from hats.com—a web site I "just have to check out." He had a book—*Commercial Aviation Safety*—open most of the trip, but I never saw him turn a page. An airplane mechanic would recognize the irony of reading about plane crashes on a plane.

Mondo is thirty-two years old. He's been married for twelve years and coaches a little league baseball team. He's been to France, Germany, and Austria—which he thinks is the most beautiful place in the world. He was stationed in Italy the longest, but the only thing he can still say in Italian is "extra tomato sauce and cheese."

After a while, I apologetically said, "I need to get some work done," and got out my laptop. After letting me finish a sentence, Mondo asked, "What are you working on?"

I briefly considered saying anything other than what it was, but I answered truthfully, "It's a sermon I'm writing for Sunday."

He said, "You're a preacher."

I had no choice. "Yes, I am."

Mondo turned to the twenty-something women across the aisle and said, "Hey, I got a preacher sitting right here."

The blonde one (no offense intended, that's what color her hair was) responded, "You're lying."

Mondo said, "Ask him."

She asked, "Are you really a preacher?" as though I had claimed to be a pro tennis star or CIA agent.

"Why would I lie?"

"What kind of church?" Mondo asked.

"One of the really good ones."

"Is it Assembly of God or Pentecostal or what?"

"It's a Baptist church."

The blonde asked, "Do you know Tim LaHaye? I haven't read anything by him, but my mother says he's really good."

"No, I haven't met Tim LaHaye."

When the excitement over a real live preacher finally died down, Mondo said, "Let me tell you a story. I was in Saudi Arabia during the Gulf War. I loaded bombs on planes. I was only under fire once, but there was a moment when I thought I was going to die.

"When I was coming home, my mom said my uncle was going to meet me at the airport. I didn't think much about it. My uncle is my mother's only brother. He's quiet. I knew he had volunteered for Vietnam, but he never said a word about it. I figured he must not have seen anything worth mentioning.

"When I got off the plane, my uncle was there with a color guard, holding a flag. Four Vietnam veterans were with him. I had never seen my uncle in his uniform. He was standing there wearing big-time medals—the Army Cross with Valor, a Purple Heart with Valor. He had been nominated for the Medal of Honor. During hand-to-hand fighting, he pulled five wounded guys out of the line of fire and was shot himself. It must have been like a movie. For the first time, he gave me a salute and I saluted him back.

"I asked him, 'Why did you go to all this trouble?'

"He said, 'Everyone needs to be properly welcomed home. When I came home no one was waiting with a parade. I want to make sure you know that someone else understands.'

"My uncle went through the worst a war can give you, but he didn't say anything about it until he wanted me to know that someone understands. Isn't that something?"

I frequently think about Mondo—especially when I hear myself asking, "Why do we go to all this trouble?" Most of what ministers do—telling the story, teaching the faith, caring for the hurting—is the chance to make sure that other people, some of whom have been through the worst life can give you, know that someone understands.

seVen

You Make Me Feel So Young

Not everyone in your church is willing to line up in a pyramid wearing a funny hat, just to have their picture made with the pastor, but some are. Many of the most interesting people in your church are not old enough to be dull. These simple, invaluable suggestions will help ministers turn children into friends.

Know names. Avoid the temptation to call children pet names like "Buddy," "Scooter," and "Little Buzzard." In some churches, the litmus test of your skill as a pastor is the ability to tell the twins apart.

Listen carefully to children, because they ask thought-provoking questions that can be used for sermon material. "What face do you see when you pray?" "Why doesn't Jesus come to our church?" "Why aren't pastors paid more?"

Reach out and call someone. When you have a question with which a child can help, such as "What should I get my daughter for Christmas?" call and ask. Few ten-year-olds will be without an answer you can choose to ignore.

Write a note to a child. "Dear Bobby, I am glad that you and I are a part of the same church. I am especially glad during our stewardship campaign . . . ."

Learn and use really bad riddles:

What excuse did Adam give his children as to why they no longer lived in Eden? "Your mother ate us out of house and home."

What did Noah say while he was loading all the animals on the ark? "Now I herd everything."

What kind of lights did they have on the ark? They had floodlights.

How do we know Abraham was smart? He knew a Lot.

When do they play tennis in the Bible? When Joseph serves in Pharaoh's court.

What kind of man was Boaz before he got married? Ruthless.

What's the sharpest book in the Bible? Acts.

What do John the Baptist and Winnie the Pooh have in common? The same middle name.

What did Jesus have in common with the fish that swallowed Jonah? Jesus had dinner with a sinner and the fish had a sinner for dinner.

Shophar Lessons

Vacation Bible School is a great time for ministers to enjoy children. The hot trend is "biblical times" curriculum. Students and teachers wear ancient Palestinian garb and eat bland bread. Pastors should quickly volunteer to be the head rabbi and get to start the day by hearing a mighty blast from a ram's horn and shouting "Sh'ma Yisra-eil, Adonai Ehloheinu, Adonai, Eh-had" which is translated, "Kids, get quiet. It's time to start Vacation Bible School."

Teaching a little Hebrew is a good way to remember how little Hebrew you remember. Explaining Passover, Pentecost, and the Feast of Weeks is easier once you are comfortable describing them as weeklong campouts.

Listen carefully to your churchyard of ancient Palestinians and you might hear:

"The ancient Palestinians really knew how to make Kool-aid."

"Can I have a bobby pin for my yarmulke?"

"We should have bought Havdalah candles that won't blow out."

"If the tax collector were really rich he wouldn't have to wear a bathrobe."

"She may be a professional musician but she really needs shophar lessons."

"*Chaverim* means 'you good buddies.'"

"Aleph, beth, gimel, daleth, phooey, I don't need to know this."

"The dreidle is for entertainment purposes only—no wagering."

"I lost a shekel in the coke machine."

"This is symbolic of something I've forgotten."

Tweety Bird: Male or Female?

Chaperoning children's camp is a better option for wealthy middle-aged people who pay big bucks to spend a week at working ranches. They have seen *City Slickers* and think that if they work hard in primitive, demanding, unpredictable conditions they will learn something about themselves and rediscover their inner child. They should save their money. At children's camp they may learn the subtle difference between the Backstreet Boys and N'Sync; to play "I Spy" and never "Truth or Dare"; how to sing the "Doxology" to the tune of *The Flintstones*; that s'mores, hayrides, and bunk beds are better in theory than practice; to take up the flashlights before lights out; that the old person should be quarterback for both teams; that *Star Wars* is in with at least one kid; not to tell the story of Shadrach, Meshach, and Abednego while sitting around the campfire; that asking whether Tweety Bird is male or female takes care of twenty minutes.

Children's camp raises important questions: What do we miss if we always sleep on comfortable beds and shower with water pressure? How are we impoverished if we never eat a food we can't identify? (I once won "Name that entrée" with the guess "Spam quesadillas.") How is our education incomplete if we spend all our time with licensed drivers?

Spongebobforlife

One of the primary purposes of children is to make youth seem human. I am—and it's hard to write—the parent of a teenager. When Carol and I had our firstborn we were delighted. As the years passed, we enjoyed talking to Graham and he enjoyed talking to us. We understood him and he understood us. We spoke the same language and liked the same music. He wanted to be around us more than he wanted to be around anyone else in the world. Much of that changed thirteen years after his birth, more than a year ago now.

We no longer speak the same language. I'm cool enough to know what cool means, but only recently did I learn that cool is no longer cool. If you're cool you say "off the chain," "tight," "freak," "sweet," or "krunk"—which I cannot find in Webster's.

We no longer like the same music. Every day as we drive to school, my teenager and I take turns picking a song. When it's my day to choose we listen to Frank Sinatra, Bruce Springsteen, Jimmy Buffett, and other classics. Graham enjoys the "music"—and I use that word loosely—of Ludacris, Good Charlotte, No Doubt, Weezer, and 50 Cent. When he is at home he enjoys this "music" through headphones.

Carol and I are no longer the people to whom our son most wants to talk. He spends some portion of most days on the computer "instant messaging"—trading short notes—with friends. Teenagers in our church who look normal have screen names like Crazymonkey, Twizzlerbear, Sweetandsour, Soccerchick, Iceman,

Flyingwhiteguy, Patheticbum, Spongebobforlife, Rockingpinkpoodle, Doorknob, Bigdogru1too, and my favorite, Ahmyheadisgone. When Carol or I ask, "What did you do at school today?" the usual response is "nothing." And yet, unsupervised my child would spend hours recounting his day to Crazymonkey.

fo sheezy

Churches need youth ministers because it's easy for teenagers and normal people to ignore one another. The best youth ministers are those whose entry into adulthood seems delayed but probable. The most important criteria for choosing a youth minister is that he or she be capable of recognizing the point at which the pastor will stop defending the youth minister.

Pastors want youth ministers to get along with the youth because many pastors find it easier to make friends with an adult the youth like than to actually make friends with the youth themselves. It's a good start, but ministers still need to make genuine attempts at conversation with youth.

Ask questions that imply that you know more than you do. For example, "Do you use Knox gelatin to get it to spike that way?" From time to time, I try to speak their language. A few years ago a youth suggested I use the phrase "It's all that and a bag of chips." My mistake was that I was so successful initially that I used this phrase well beyond its one-week expiration date. From this experience I learned to communicate by making fun of my inability to communicate. I have recently begun saying "dog" (dawg) around our youth. As far as I can tell, "dog" can be a compliment or an insult, a noun or a verb. (None of this knowledge is of any use to you, because if I know it, then it's way too old for a youth to actually use.) When I say, "Don't be dogging me, dog," I sound so hopelessly out of touch that it's amusing—at least to me. "Props" is another word I use to indicate that I know I'm out of date. "Props," I believe, means accolades or credit. When I say, "Give the dog his props, fo sheezy" (I don't have a clue on "fo sheezy," but I've heard it several times), I am obviously too old and cool to be cool.

The impermanency of what is considered cool is the reason you should not give in to the temptation to get a tattoo as a way of relating. (A discreet dove on your toe might be okay.)

Don't pierce anything you don't want to pierce. Ears are generally accepted spots for female ministers, but someone will question every other spot.

Show your hipness by writing new verses for "Kum Ba Yah"— e.g., "Someone's bowling, Lord." The motions write themselves. Find "mad" (it means "good") missions projects: Youth like painting buildings, delivering meals to senior citizens, supervising children's games, and rollerblading for missions inside the sanctuary. They tend to shy away from anything involving listening to anyone more than twenty-five years of age who can't use "fo sheezy" in a sentence.

A Brief Respite from Sanity

If all else fails—and my hands are shaking as I type this—consider going to youth camp. In general, prospective ministers should read their job descriptions carefully, looking for the line that says "the pastor will go to youth camp each summer." In business terms this is a deal-breaker. Before you accept such a contingency, ask, "Do I want to join extremely young people and only a few truly adult sponsors for five days without long pants?"

These are completely acceptable excuses for missing youth camp:

"I need a silent, individual prayer retreat."

"My own child will feel uncomfortable if I am are there."

"Someone else's child will feel uncomfortable if I am there."

"I can't be away from my church/family/sanity that long."

If in a praiseworthy, though misguided, attempt to relate to your youth, you take the drastic step of actually attending youth camp, you will learn so much.

You will learn that you are prehistoric. At thirty-five I entered a three-on-three basketball tournament. Early in the game, when I was still running, I tried to steal the ball. A young punk warned his teammate by yelling "Old guy!" The high point came when the kid I was pretending to guard asked how old I was. When I answered "fifty-seven," he responded, "You're not bad for fifty-seven."

You cannot find a bunk in which you can sleep. You will end up next to a counselor who snores loud—freight train, earthquake, and hibernating grizzly loud.

You may be surprised to learn that Lovin' Spoonful is popular again. (Maybe there's hope for Barry Manilow.)

If you get up at seven you will always have hot water, but the older you get the more sleep you need.

After four days it seems perfectly normal to eat French fries at every meal.

Don't participate in the talent show unless you have a talent. You may think this is obvious but it wasn't to me—don't dance if there is a video camera in the room.

Ah la vis ma ha ta turka klappa nu

After a few days, some things at camp will seem almost amusing, but none of this is to be tried at home!

You may smile at unfortunate incidents involving shaving cream, Saran Wrap, and baby oil, but do not begin to believe that the amused-by-water-guns person you are at camp is the real you.

The chorus for one of the five hundred praise choruses I've sung is "Na-na-na-na-na-na-na-na-na-na-na-na." I should not suggest this for the processional hymn at my church.

I should not try to wake myself up in the morning like the youth at First Baptist Church, Austin, Texas, do. They first sing "If you're happy and you know it" in Swedish, "Ah la vis ma ha ta turka klappa nu." (Try it.) Each person quickly pours a cup of coffee into a cup of ice and chug-a-lugs it as fast as possible. I was once invited to give a brief speech ("You people are like skydivers to me") and join them. It wakes you up, but if you do this at home you will feel stupid.

One of my clearest "this is not the real me" experiences was serving as the unenthusiastic coach for Monday Mega-madness—a ten-stage relay race. We threw our shoes into the center, ran to the middle, put on our shoes, and ran back. Pairs of participants sat on one another's feet and inched their way to the center. The boys formed a circle around the girls and ran to the center. Two participants from each team ran to the center and spun around a baseball bat ten times. We jumped on the ground and formed a flat pyramid. The team lay on the ground side by side and rolled one person, the "surfer," to the inside. (I wish I was making this up). Two players rode piggyback to the center, then carried a third on a wet towel to the center. Each team member stepped through a Hula Hoop while holding hands. For a few isolated seconds I almost enjoyed Monday Mega-madness, but I was more than happy to skip Wacky Water Wednesday.

Ministers come back from camp with unpleasant memories of extracting marbles with your toes from a wading pool filled with pancake batter, but when you come back in one piece, count it the grace of God.

Bungee Jump Bible Studies

Studies show that people between the ages of eighteen and twenty-two watch *The Matrix* more often than they go to church. This does not lessen the minister's responsibility to reach out to young scholars. Many universities with religious affiliations make this easy by providing a time for churches to share who they are with incoming students.

When I was the pastor of College Heights Baptist Church in Manhattan, Kansas, a small Christian college invited pastors to meet incoming students and give a ninety-second commercial. The freshmen were divided into six groups, so the nine ministers who showed up gave their spiels six times.

The first time we all said the same things—our names, what church we represented, worship times, and directions.

The second time through the parade of pastors the commercials became competitive. At first it was just location—"My church is the closest"—followed by "My church is a beautiful scenic drive away."

During the third round the competition shifted to food. I innocently started it when I said, "We'll be serving breakfast on Sunday."

The next minister said, "We'll have lunch"—as if to suggest their lunch would be better than our breakfast.

A third minister tried to top us both: "We'll have dinner"—as if dinner is the most important meal of the day.

A desperate minister tried for the athletic vote: "We play softball."

A second countered, "We play volleyball."

A third retaliated, "We water ski."

I would not have been surprised to hear, "We have a bungee jump Bible study."

Then the music portion of the tournament began. One promised, "We don't sing hymns. We'll never have any music you can't tap your toe to."

"We have a bass guitar."

"We have drums, so there."

"We have mariachis, tambourines, and a sousaphone, nyah, nyah, nyah."

About the fifth time through, the co-pastor at First Baptist said, "All of our churches have most things in common, but at our church my wife preaches half of the time." Then he shouted, "So if you're interested in women come to First Baptist." A few freshmen woke up.

Near the end, the pastors united against the ministers who weren't there. The pastor of the Church of Christ gave directions saying, "You'll have to go past Grace Baptist, but you don't want to stop there anyway." Then he apologized, "I'm sorry. I shouldn't have said that."

One of the other ministers shouted, "Take another shot." I don't do immature stuff like that anymore.

On my last turn I went for the jugular: "At our church we serve free food all of the time. You'll meet scads of good-looking eighteen-year-olds. When the offering plate is passed we encourage college students to take money out."

Lutheran Highlighters

For five incoming freshman classes, I was the pastor of Lake Shore Baptist in Waco, Texas. I have never been to a snake handling, an Ernest Ansley revival, or to Lourdes to see the crutches piled high, but I have been to the world's most bizarre religious gathering—church rush at Baylor University's Welcome Week. Each August I joined representatives from seventy-five churches in trying to retain our dignity while wooing incoming students into visiting our churches. Just inside the basketball arena a huge sign directed Baptists to the right and non-Baptists to the left. (Was this a subtle allusion to the sheep and the goats?) Bleary-eyed students circled church displays to decide if they wanted to risk a conversation with someone who could be a minister. The church representatives pitched their ecclesiastical wares like carnival barkers: "Step right up. We've got the church for you."

The giveaways are magnificent. In a single day I picked up two Lutheran highlighters, a Methodist candy bar, a Church of Christ pen, nondenominational chewing gum, Assembly of God ministerial trading cards, a Bible Church bookmark, Episcopalian peppermints, and every flavor of Baptist Jolly Ranchers. I am to this day the proud owner of a green and gold (Baylor's colors) rosary. One minister surveying the scene commented, "If someone with a whip of cords starts kicking over tables, I'm getting out of here."

In their handouts churches promised a home away from home, a church "on the grow," a breath of fresh air, a place of refuge, a place to play, innovative worship, contemporary worship, contemporary praise, contemporary music, contemporary Bible study, expository Bible study, expository preaching, very little preaching, *Escuela Dominical followed by Servicio de Adoracion*, anointed ministry, guitars, hand bells, liturgical dance, puppets, large groups, small groups, one-to-one discipleship, e-mail communication, tailgate parties, concerts, movies, bowling, tubin', fishing, ski trips, pool tournaments, dance contests, a wooden token that can be taken to the church and redeemed for a 22-ounce insulated mug, pizza, and hamburgers. (Wouldn't it be wonderful if we had church rush for hungry people?)

My church's tasteful display consisted of communion table paraments and a tactful sign—"Have more questions than answers? Prefer conversation to lecture?"—that invited students to our college Sunday school class. I was, nonetheless, willing to consider "Register here to win a green and gold sports car."

Homecoming Weekend

If ministers get into a conversation with a college student about why he or she should come to church they need to have reasons ready:

"You don't have to take your roommate."

"Most churches will feed you once a week. Wednesday suppers are cheaper than the appetizers alone at Chili's."

"Long pants are fun to wear every once in a while."

"Churches don't charge admission."

"On Homecoming weekend, you will want to take your parents to a church where people will act like they know you. We'll play along."

She Told Us So

Most churches in university towns try advertising in the school paper. This is as productive as Jerry Falwell running ads in *The Village Voice*. If you, nonetheless, still feel so led, try to be clever:

God wants you to come to our church.
She told us so.

Still looking for the perfect match?
Ecumenically minded,
theologically inclusive,
ministry-committed congregation
looking for fun-loving college students.
Must be willing to explore new ideas.

Looking for a church like your mother's?
We're not it.

Last Sunday morning,
51% of college students hung out,
19% stayed in bed till noon,
18% can't remember what they did,
9% washed the car,
2% studied,
and less than 1% went to church.
Be a radical.

"Nothing is more irritating than a good example." —Mark Twain
Irritate your roommates. Go to church this Sunday.

"Has any religious group ever expressed concern that they were
boring God?" —Roy Blount, Jr.
At our church, we're trying not to bore God.

Students who plan to be doctors, ministers, photographers,
accountants, social workers, teachers, artists, and newscasters are
fun to talk to. If you're a married minister, the sophomore who
thinks it's time to consider dating may inexplicably look to you as
an expert in this area. Offer Christian pickup lines: "My prayers are
answered—is this pew taken?" "What do you think Paul meant by
that holy kiss stuff?" "I love a good love offering." Relate by referring
to finals as Armageddon and suggesting that in Genesis 1 God may
have waited for five days and then pulled an all-nighter. Talking to
people who know that their life is ahead of them helps us recognize
that some of our greatest joys are yet to be.

Illegal Hand Signals

Sometimes the only people who make us feel younger than children,
youth, and college students make us feel are senior citizens. Every
pastor needs elderly friends. Take communion to the homebound,
call on people you enjoy, collect life stories, and enjoy visiting nursing homes.

I will not win a Nobel Prize, sing at Carnegie Hall, or climb
Mount Everest, but I don't worry about all that I won't accomplish,
because I have been a judge at a Senior Bible Quiz. Each year the
Central Texas Senior Ministry sponsors a Bible quiz for the resi-
dents of several nursing homes. A month before the event,
participants are given eight pages to study. In a manner similar to a
spelling bee, contestants are removed from the line after missing

two questions. Ribbons are given to the top three finishers. Just as in the ancient Olympics, the competition is about glory rather than monetary gain. (The woman who complained about the absence of trophies did not reflect the attitude of most competitors.)

Several contestants kissed the congeniality award good-bye early on. The trash-talking surprised me. The nursing home that didn't show "chickened out." One woman repeatedly stuck out her tongue. Another kept trying to call time on the other competitors by saying, "ding, ding, ding." Some muttered about illegal hand signals. When the head official asked, "Will you be friends when this is over?" Ann, a delightful woman who took the silver, replied, "We weren't friends before."

I wish that, like an Olympic judge, I could have given style points to the contestants who said: "I would have won last year, but I fell asleep." "There's a lot more pressure up here than sitting down there." "I really could use a short-term memory."

The gladiators knew their stuff. I was glad to have the answers in front of me. You know the old saying, "Those who cannot remember the Beatitudes, judge." The competitor who took the gold, Isador, went twenty rounds without missing a question and had no expectation of ever missing.

One of the verses that they memorized was Psalm 119:105, "Thy word is a lamp unto my feet and a light unto my path." While there are elements of *Jeopardy* at the Senior Bible Quiz, this wasn't Bible trivia (which could be considered an oxymoron). On some questions the participants tried to remember what they had studied that morning, but on others they tried to express what they had learned seventy years ago.

Thirty years from now, when my generation starts taking our place in nursing homes, the crowd that shows up for the Senior Bible Quiz will be smaller. There aren't many dog-eared, underlined Inclusive New Revised Standard Versions with notes in the margin. Ministers need to celebrate people of all ages who have found a story older than they are—whether for the first time or the thousandth.

(eight)

About Four Seasons

Early Christians thought a period of fervent preparation should precede the Christmas festival. These days became "Advent," which is loosely translated "shopping days." As Christmas gets close many preachers hide in their studies because they are afraid of what's out there. Ministers are sensitive spiritual beings uncomfortable with the materialism at the mall. Large men with white beards are pushing terrified three-year-olds to sit on their laps. Truly awful parodies of Christmas carols ("three turtle necks, two French toasts") are playing—with accordion accompaniment. Visa cards are melting. The drive for perfect gifts, perfect parties, and perfect worship services leads to perfect migraines. Christmas becomes a consumer-driven, sentiment-dripping pain in the neck. Ministers aren't surprised that the wise men, the only ones who brought gifts, were late for Christmas, but here are a few simple suggestions on how ministers can enjoy rather than endure the season.

Give small, personalized gifts (e.g., copies of sermons) to members early in December. Some will reciprocate by giving you presents. (Unfortunately it can be difficult to return "Precious Moments" figurines.)

Share a Nativity set with children (it doesn't matter if they are your own or someone else's). Encourage the smallest child to hide the baby Jesus. Use this as a clever sermon illustration.

Wear your bathrobe to church and claim you're playing a shepherd. Retell the story: "The cold wind made the shepherds too miserable to notice how hungry they were, but the youngest shepherd suggested they sing some old shepherd songs. The oldest shepherd reminded him that they hated old shepherd songs. They told a few jokes that cannot be repeated in church . . . ."

Ask several deacons if they get a big Christmas bonus where they work.

If you have to preach too often in December, start the traditions of Lessons and Carols, a Moravian Love Feast, or a figgy pudding dance.

Advent Shmadvent

As the pastor of a church with liturgical worship, you might guess that I get questions from young ministers concerning Advent. These might be examples of some such e-mail correspondence.

To: Pastor, Liturgical Church
From: A Young Minister
    What's the deal with Advent?

To: Young Minister
From: Your Guide to Advent
    The word Advent comes from the Latin *advenire*, which means "coming" or "going."

To: Rev. High Church
From: Rev. Low Church
> The deacons got into an argument over which candle to light on the Second Sunday of Advent. We have three yellows and two greens left.

To: Rev. LC
From: Keeping the Candles Burning
> Light whatever works for you.

To: Mr. Liturgy
From: Counting Days
> Advent is going great. We even have a sign out in front of the church that says "19 Shopping Days Left in Advent."

To: Shopping Liturgist
From: Also Shopping
> I'm delighted that Advent is going so well.

To: Adventurer
From: Needing Money for Gifts
> Who started Advent? I've got a ten spot riding on the Seventh Day Adventists.

To: Gambler
From: Grateful to Gregory
> It was Pope Gregory I (590–604), who I do not believe was a Seventh Day Adventist. Don't make any more wagers. Advent shouldn't be about losing money.

To: Father Christmas
From: Wondering
> I have been following the Scriptures for Advent and am disappointed. The texts deal with judgment and repentance. Why is Advent such a downer? Why can't we read about Christmas?

To: Wanderer
From: Wishing You a Roman Holiday
It's Pope Sylvester II's fault. Before his reign (999–1003), Advent was schizophrenic. In France and Germany, Advent was spent fasting. Meanwhile, the church in Italy celebrated Advent as four weeks of parties. Sylvester, unfortunately, went with the less joyful Advent.

To: Italian-at-heart Friend
From: Guessing It's Forbearing
We got into another argument at the last deacons' meeting. We know that the Advent themes include hope, peace, and love, but is the fourth theme forbearance, self-control, or self-esteem?

To: Forbearing One
From: Joyful One
You're right.

To: Self-appointed Expert
From: What To Do?
Everyone but Mrs. Wendleken is on board with Advent. During the lighting of the candles she mutters under her breath, "Advent Shmadvent."

To: Advent Friend
From: Merry Advent!
Leave a lump of coal in her Advent stocking.

"Now Listen to My Story . . ."

Several Decembers ago, my gifted friend Harry Wooten, Minister of Music at Royal Lane Baptist Church, Dallas, Texas, reminded me that he has a peculiar mind and too much time on his hands. (Harry says his friend Michael Dell deserves the blame for this, but I'm guessing Michael would rather be left out.) Harry shared a list of Christmas carols to be sung to the tunes of television theme songs. After adding a simple script, I was delighted with the childlike wonder with which much of our congregation responded to the following:

An Addams Family Christmas

We experience Christmas in a variety of ways—through Scripture, literature, and art. The most important way in which we feel the hope of Advent is music. Tonight we'll be subjected to the magic of the season through the story in song. Gifted yuletide singers will share beloved Christmas classics.

"O Come O Come Emmanuel" to the tune of *I Love Lucy*

Did you recognize the tune? By joining Israel's hope for ransom with Desi's love for Lucy, the hymn takes on an international quality. Our second Advent hymn comes from the book of Isaiah, written 800 years before Christ—a creepy, crawly time.

"Lo How a Rose" to the tune of *The Addams Family*

The rose, the blossom bright in the cold of winter, surprises us like the Addams Family, like Morticia bringing light as well as darkness wherever she goes. Our story moves to a pasture, a field that was in Palestine, but that could have been anywhere—in North Texas, for instance.

"While Shepherds Watched" to the tune of *Dallas*

The parallels between Herod the Great and J. R. Ewing are clear. This story takes place amid wars and rumors of wars.

"Hark the Herald Angels Sing" to the tune of *M*A*S*H**

In this paraphrase, Hawkeye is a shepherd and Winchester is a wise man. Hot Lips doesn't have a part. Jesus was born long, long ago, far, far away.

"Angels, from the Realms of Glory" to the tune of *Star Wars*

Is Herod the Great more like J. R. Ewing or Darth Vader? The joyous story is heard even in faraway Florida. I think it was Florida, but I'm not old enough to remember this show.

"Child in the Manger" to the tune of *Flipper*

We end where we began, overlooking a little town of hills and stars, a town where poor mountaineers barely kept their families fed.

"O Little Town of Bethlehem" to the tune of *The Beverly Hillbillies*

The spiritual interpretation of this magical musical event may seem unnecessary. The theological significance of singing classic Christmas carols to old TV theme songs is clear, but at the risk of stating the obvious, here it is. At Christmas, church people feel like someone has stolen our words and set them to the wrong tunes. Walking through the mall and hearing the strains of "O Come All Ye Faithful" seems odd. Turning on the radio and hearing Madonna— not the good one—singing "Silent Night" is peculiar. When we feel that what's ours has been stolen, we need to remember that it's not ours. The story of Jesus is for shepherds keeping watch over their flock by night, Cuban bandleaders, creepy people, oil barons, Koreans, imperial storm troopers, marine biologists, people in the Tennessee hills and Beverly Hills, and everyone who has hopes and fears.

Brett Younger

Liturgical Games

Most ministers are proficient with most of the church year. They know Advent (countdown to Christmas), Epiphany (take down the decorations), Lent (get depressed, lose a few pounds), Easter (get happy, gain a few pounds), Pentecost (wear your red outfit), and Ordinary Time (which is as exciting as its name; a good time to preach a long series). We know how to handle unofficial high holy days like Mother's Day (conservative churches give carnations to the mother with the most children; liberal churches give carnations to everyone who has ever nurtured anyone) and Father's Day (ignore it). What ministers often forget is that church members operate with different seasons. Pastors need insightful responses to baseball, football, and basketball seasons.

Bread, Wine, Peanuts, and Cracker Jacks

When we begin the season of Lent, our minds turn to the spiritual disciplines—prayer, fasting, Scripture reading, meditation, and baseball. Lent is from *lencten*, the Anglo-Saxon word for "spring." Scholars speculate that "Lent" is a shortened version of "spring training." Lent begins with Ash Wednesday (near the beginning of college baseball) and ends the day before Easter (after the big leagues have started).

The spiritual aspects of baseball are undeniable. The goal is to be "safe" (saved) until you can go "home" (God's eternal presence). Watching a baseball game is following the psalmist's admonition: "Be still." In a world that's too busy, baseball is countercultural—sit, relax, and reflect. The mystic Yogi Berra pointed out baseball's contemplative qualities, "90 percent of the game is half mental."

Unlike other sports, baseball is timeless. No clock counts down the seconds. People who complain that baseball is slow miss the point—dreams are slow; growth is slow; spirituality is slow. The great Yogi put it, "It ain't over till it's over." Some of the elements of the game change (try not to think about the abominations of artificial turf and designated hitters), but baseball itself is eternal.

Lent is a time to pay attention, so look at the angle of the bat, the ball no bigger than a grape traveling as fast as a bullet, and the ballet of the fielders diving. Watch all the back-bending, knee-stretching, and torso-revolving that goes on in the on-deck circle. See how stepping into the batter's box is a ritual unto itself for slow-moving players. Watch how frequently and forcefully ballplayers spit and how involved they are with dirt—rubbing dirt into their gloves, tossing dirt to test the wind, and tapping dirt off their spikes with their bat. "You can observe a lot by watching," Yogi Berra said.

During Lent, listen for the crack of wood (the ping of aluminum isn't the same) and the whack of horsehide hitting leather. Listen to the college boy behind you discover that he can't marry his date because she doesn't understand the infield fly rule and to the ten-year-old in front of you describe his plans to chase every foul ball as if it were gold.

Smell the Lent, the spring, the green, green grass that has been seeded, watered, fussed over, and coddled like a putting green. Taste the goodness of the holy season, hot dogs that would seem dull served on a plate, but which, dripping with mustard, taste like manna from heaven at a ball game. Join the choir singing the "Star-spangled Banner and "Take Me Out to the Ballgame." Hope for stolen bases, double plays, and more knuckleball pitchers, but lean forward only on 3-2 counts.

Even so, remember that Lent is a time for penitence. "We made too many wrong mistakes" (Yogi). Believe the promise of Numbers 15:28, "The priest shall make atonement before the Lord for the one who commits an error." Bartlett Giamatti writes, "Baseball breaks your heart. It is designed to break your heart. The game begins in the spring, when everything else begins again, and it blossoms in the summer, filling the afternoons and evenings, and then as soon as the chill rains come, it stops, and leaves you to face the fall alone."

God speaks to different people through different disciplines. Long ago I passed the point where the oldest players are younger than I am, but baseball continues to make me feel alive. It's a sign of hope that when life is loud and rushed, there is still baseball. I suppose it's possible to feel the cool breeze of the Spirit at a basketball game or imagine Jesus at a football game, but neither seems as likely to me.

Jacques Barzun wrote, "Whoever wants to know the heart and mind of America had better learn baseball." Would it be too much to say, "Whoever wants to know the heart and mind of God had better learn baseball?" Yes, of course it would, but take your soul to a ball game and give thanks to the God of Abraham, Isaac, and Jacob, Willie, Mickey, and the Duke, the God of bread and wine, peanuts and Cracker Jacks, the God of grace and glory, shoestring catches and curve balls, the God of the baptistery and the pitcher's mound, and the God of new wineskins and old baseball fans.

The Goalposts of Life

I was the pastor of a faculty-filled Baptist church in Waco, Texas, for five football seasons. I graduated from Baylor University. I went to football games. And yet I was never asked to pray before a game. What could be the problem? I don't understand how I could continually be overlooked. Nonetheless, I keep working on the prayer I will offer before a Baylor football game if I'm ever asked. (Feel free to use this prayer, as I'm not holding my breath.)

> God, we give you thanks that football is just a game—only in part because we're not that good at it. On occasion, our defense parts like the Red Sea and our quarterback's passes are not always as true as King David's sling. We are tempted to point out what a fine witness it would be if the world's largest Baptist university wins this battle, Lord, but we will not. We ask only that you help the Baptist boys play so well that the ones who are not Baptist will wish they were. We are grateful, of course, that Baylor is not a football factory like some schools.
>
> Nonetheless, we pray for patience, Lord. We haven't had a winning season in, well, Lord, not even Job suffered this long. God, as a Baylor alum, class of '83, I remember the glorious days when Mike Singletary roamed the holy ground of this stadium and beseech Thee to raise up another helmet-cracker.

We pray for sportsmanship. May there be no unnecessary late hits. If any players aren't attending classes, we pray that their conscience and/or the NCAA may smite them mightily.

God, we feel funny asking for protection for these players. If you choose to play a game in which 300-pounders collide at great speed, aren't you taking your life and cartilage into your own hands? We pray anyway that if any players on the other team should be hurt that their injuries will not keep them out of any game beyond this one.

God, as we sneak a peak at the luxurious sky boxes, we briefly wonder if they have a place at a university that claims allegiance to one who had no place to lay his head. We wonder if Jesus could attend a university that charges this much a semester hour. We consider confessing the evil of spending big bucks on football when people are starving, but then we think better of that.

Most of all, God, we ask forgiveness for treating prayer as an inconsequential part of pre-game festivities—less important than the marching band and the coin toss. How can we cheapen something so holy as prayer?

We pray that no one will mistake what happens before football games for prayer at its most genuine. If the only prayers people hear are the kind prayed in stadiums, why would anyone ever pray?

Help us remember, O God, that real prayer seldom takes place over a loudspeaker. As we run toward the goalposts of life, teach us that prayer is not an empty ritual, but opening our lives to you. Amen.

Double Dribbling

Many ministers have not realized the sacred aspects of hoops. Baseball stirs poets and football leads to prayer, but I've been inspired attending basketball games involving six-year-olds. My son, Caleb, was on a team sponsored by a local pizza place. His brother delighted in calling them the "Delivery Boys."

The referees are extremely important to six-year-olds' basketball, because they have to point players in the right direction, as in, "Go that way!" or "Go the other way!" Players shoot at the wrong goal once or twice a game, but fortunately the kids who shoot at the wrong goal are also the ones most likely to miss.

The referees help teams throw the ball in bounds. Getting one player to stand out of bounds to toss the ball in is harder than you would guess. The other four players gather in a clump and beg for the ball. "Throw it to me."

"No, throw it to me and I'll be your best friend."

"Throw it to me and I'll throw it right back. I promise."

Other than throwing the ball in bounds, which is primarily a test of friendship, passing is an as yet undiscovered art. Most passes are dribbles that get away—which isn't surprising since most dribbles are five feet off the ground. When players show any inclination to pass, and sometimes when they don't, the others start yelling. The farther they are from the basket, the louder they shout and wave their arms. The ball handler responds by tossing the ball aimlessly into the air. The few passes that arrive at their intended destination are of six inches or less.

Defense is limited—only in part because it's against the rules to steal the ball when a player is dribbling. At the beginning of each quarter the coach tells each player the number of the player he or she is to guard. This leads to running around to see the numbers on the backs of the opposing teams' jerseys. Players who are guarded closely take it personally. One player repeatedly shouted, "Go away" to the boy guarding him. Another appealed for help, "Mom, he won't stop guarding me."

One of the nice things about six-year-olds' basketball games is that no one keeps score. I was embarrassed when a woman asked me what the score was after a game. I answered, "We're not supposed to keep score."

"What was the score?"

"28-24." Why would she think that about me?

You see some things that you don't see at other games: a player going to the water fountain during play; the toss for the jump ball bouncing; a coach using a timeout to tie shoes; a coach sternly warning his players, "Don't stand under the basket. The ball will hit you on the head."

The most disturbing aspect for basketball aficionados is the frequency of traveling. Double dribbling is legal, so on almost every trip down the court players walk with the ball.

Legalizing double dribbling is helpful for children who haven't played competitive basketball. It is, however, frustrating for six-year-olds who've played with older brothers for years. In our driveway we call traveling. No one, not even a six-year-old, gets to walk with the ball.

All of this led to a moment of great pride. Caleb was dribbling down the court when one of his teammates almost ran into him, so he stopped dribbling. The other players were either far away under the goal, had their backs turned, or were uninterested. Let me say without even a trace of humility that any other six-year-old on the court would have begun dribbling again, but Caleb wouldn't do it. His teammates shouted for him to dribble. His coach said, "Dribble." Someone on the sidelines shouted, "Dribble, Caleb." My boy knew it was wrong. He stood there with a determined look on his face and held the ball until the other team took it away from him. I couldn't have been prouder. I had a vision that one day my son will be twenty or thirty or forty and someone or everyone will encourage him to take a shortcut, and he'll say, "That's not what I learned. I'm not going to do it."

In all that we do, in every season from Advent to hoops, the church is trying to be the people who would rather let the other team steal the ball than give up their principles.

(nine)

April's Fool

What do people expect from a church newsletter? Everyone wants news about upcoming events, updates on members, crossword puzzles, recipes, and fishing tips, but beyond that we're not sure. Ministers write columns on anything and everything—why they are Episcopal, why they are not Episcopal, something cute one of their children did, and something cute they imagined their child doing. Amazingly, newsletters are still as interesting as a zip code directory. In my experience, the one issue that families fight to read first is the one filled with the pastor's lies. This chapter will make putting together your April Fools' newsletter as easy as 1, 2, 3—except the list goes to 30.

(1) *Use poetry.* April 1 is usually during Lent. I'm no Ruth Bell Graham, but here's a poem you're welcome to use:

Lent is
Taking time, creating a space
In the midst of the hectic
Clutter of our lives.
Lent is six weeks,

Just a little too long to give up
Sugar or television or red meat
Without the novelty of it
Wearing thin by the end.
This year let's give up fried eggs.
Scrambling them will be
A little more trouble,
But not much.

(2) *Promote educational activities.*
Book Study 1
On Wednesday at 6:30, Vicki Kabat, the mother of three sons, will share from her book, *Momsense*. Vicki, like a growing number of Presbyterians, is a snake-handler. Her presentation will include rattlesnakes, copperheads, and water moccasins.

(3) *Challenge the people.*
Book Study 2
The next tome for the book group will be *Das Wesen des Christentums* by Adolf Harnack.

(4) *Keep members informed.*
Called Business Meeting
On Wednesday evening following supper we will vote on:
(a) roller-skating in the fellowship hall on Saturday evenings.
(b) discontinuing coffee on Sunday mornings.
(c) a new stained-glass window—John the Baptist's head on a platter for the window next to the kitchen.
(d) a recommendation that staff appreciation week be extended to a month.

(5) *Publicize fellowship events.*
Golf Tournament
The third annual competition between our church and the Jewish temple will be this Saturday. We are tired of losing so we are bring-

ing in three ringers. (This will cost an extra $5 each.) They are going by the names "Tom," "Dick," and "Harry." We will claim that they started attending our church three months ago. Contact the office if you have any silly qualms about this.

(6) *Apologize for mistakes.*
Corrections
In last week's newsletter under "Prayer Concerns," we printed, "Bruce Neatherlin underwent quadruple bypass surgery." We meant to put "Bruce Neatherlin got a bad haircut." We apologize for any concern this may have caused Bruce's family or friends.

In the latest version of our church cookbook, the recipe for Mary Ellen Smith's pecan pie includes "1 cup of Tabasco sauce." It should read "1 cup of sugar." We are sorry for any discomfort this may have produced.

(7) *Keep people informed about missionaries.*
An Update from Nicaragua
Donella Ware writes that she recently struck oil in her backyard in Managua. That's right—"black gold, Texas tea." Donella will soon be moving to Beverly Hills, California.

(8) *Support spirituality.*
The Practice of Prayer
Praying for financial gain will be the topic at this Monday's discussion. Judy Prather suggests participants bring their checkbooks—which they will be using for "prayer imagery."

(9) *Present options.*
Next Summer's Mission Trip
Are you tired of mission trips to places where the people are so needy? Why not go to the happiest place in the world? Would you like for next summer's trip to be to Disney World in beautiful Orlando, Florida?

(10) *Support Christian education.*
<u>Sunday School News</u>
We're changing the time for Sunday school! Every Sunday we get to church early and wait for everything to start. Since we're all already here we're going to start fifteen minutes earlier.

(11) *Encourage sacred worship.*
<u>Choir</u>
Our choir loft can only seat so many, so if you're thinking about joining the choir, don't be so sure of yourself.

(12) *Lead deacons to new ministries.*
<u>Deacon On Call</u>
Jim Creel, 776-2757
One of Jim's gifts is helping people fill out tax forms.

(13) *Raise liturgical issues.*
<u>Schedule Change</u>
Easter has been moved to the last Sunday in May. We realize this is Memorial Day weekend and are sorry for any inconvenience, but we couldn't get everything ready in time.

(14) *Promote the recreation ministry.*
<u>Sports News</u>
Our Fighting Doves softball team is undefeated. Last week we beat the Quakers 9-0 and not a peep was heard out of them. This week we play the Charismatics, so let's get excited!

(15) *Keep youth informed.*
<u>News from Your Youth Minister</u>
We're not going to summer camp this year. I'm tired of all the complaining. So there.

(16) *Help people think about giving.*
<u>Stewardship Quote of the Week</u>
Money doesn't always bring happiness. People with ten million dollars are no happier than people with nine million dollars.
—Hobart Brown

(17) *Test the kitchen staff.*
<u>Wednesday Night Menu</u>
$3—adults
$4—children

Consommé de Volaille à la Chiffonade
Chiffonade Soup

Petits Soufflés de Homard
Individual Lobster Soufflés

Scharzhofberger
Moselle – White

Filet de Boeuf en Croûte
Tenderloin of Beef in Pastry

Pommard, Les Ápenots
Red Burgundy

Pommes de Terre Allumettes
Matchstick Potatoes

Asperges aux Miettes Cirtonnées
Asparagus with Lemon Crumbs

Gâteau d'Amandes au Chocolat
Almond Chocolate Torte

(18) *Ask adults to be involved with youth.*
Youth Event
On Saturday night the youth will have a scavenger hunt. We need fast drivers, old cars, and people who know the words to the Gilligan's Island theme song.

(19) *Offer inspirational thoughts.*
Famous Theologian's Quote of the Week
"I've left a key under the mat." —from C. S. Lewis's *Notes to the Plumber*

(20) *Make up inspirational thoughts.*
Fictitious Spiritual Thought for the Day
"An appreciation of silly attempts at humor is a sign of great spiritual maturity." —Billy Graham

(21) *Use material from Christian magazines.*
The Christian Century's Scary Anagram
Britney Spears: Presbyterians

(22) *Encourage Bible reading.*
Reading the Bible through in Fifty Years Plan
This week: Leviticus 2:7-15

(23) *Present alternative forms of contemplation.*
Lectio Divina Verse of the Week
When Methuselah was one hundred and eighty-seven years old he fathered Lamech. —Genesis 5:25

(24) *Include senior adults.*
Senior Adult Poker and Potluck!

(25) *Include children.*
TABAC
Third, fourth, and fifth graders who want out of worship are welcome to join us for Thinking about Becoming a Christian.

(26) *Share uplifting correspondence.*
A Note to Our Church
Dear Church Members,
I would like to thank you for the cards and flowers, but I forgot to tell you I was in the hospital. Nevertheless, I am a
Bitter Member

(27) *Enlist help for the finance committee.*
Mathematical Skills Needed
Do you like counting money? Are you really honest? Will you take a lie detector test?

(28) *Encourage study.*
Library News
Our church librarian says, "We've got lots of books. I'm tired of begging you people to learn something. You know where we are."

(29) *Use your pastor's column to announce a change in emphasis.*
Pastoral Reflections
For decades, worshipers have come to Broadway Baptist Church because we take worship seriously by drawing on centuries of Christian tradition. We gather in a cross-shaped sanctuary with a high ceiling, arches, and stained-glass windows that call our attention to the Mystery of the Divine. We hear a magnificent organ call us to worship, sing sacred music that has lasted for generations, share in litanies like the ancient Israelites, confess our sins as the church has always done, listen for the voice of God in Holy Scripture, meditate in the silence in which the Spirit speaks, and offer our gifts and ourselves. Like many of you, I came to Broadway

because I experience reverent, holy worship as the most meaningful way in which I give myself to God.

But hey, times change.

More and more churches are moving away from sacred worship to a more entertaining approach that we've been told packs them in. They raise hard questions: Why should we stubbornly keep singing music that has been around hundreds of years when everyone else is having fun with music that will be forgotten five minutes from now? If confession and silence are fun, then why don't they have them at ball games? Why can't church be more like MTV? So Sunday, we'll start giving this new stuff a whirl!

Instead of the organ chiming the hour, an announcement over the P.A. will thunder, "Let's get ready to worshiiiiiiiiiiiiiip!" Rather than an ancient greeting, we'll say, "God loves you and I do, too," and hug.

"Right now I'm most excited about putting together a praise band," says David Keith, our Minister of Music. "We need three guitars and a drummer—just like the Beatles—and five people who look like Jennifer Lopez to stand in front and mouth the words."

Al Travis, our organist, is keyed up about our new musical directions: "Most classical music and sacred hymnody is even older than I am. I look forward to playing music that's not so polished."

Choir members like Sandy Nelson are thrilled: "Singing little choruses will be so much easier than long, complicated anthems. Choir rehearsals will be cut in half." (Of course, the choir will no longer be needed as soon as the Broadway Praise Team starts rocking.)

"Music changes," says energized young person Andy Campbell. "The time for meaningful, sacred music is over."

Our new musical style won't take much preparation, but we may not get the overhead screens up before Sunday, so we hope you'll be able to learn our opening chorus:

I will praise you.
I will praise you.
I will praise you.
(chorus) I will praise you!
(repeat 12 times)

See you Sunday. It will be awesome!

(30) *You might want to include a disclaimer.*
If you have questions or comments about this newsletter, please check the date on the front. If you still have concerns, call denominational headquarters.

(ten)

Haloes, Hell, and Hand Towels

Some ministers avoid thorny theological issues, but in the long run it is more fun to speak to these difficult questions with courage. Your church newsletter column is an opportunity to deal with hot-button issues like eternal beings, the power of the dark side, and hard-to-get-out stains.

The Idiot's Guide to Angels

Angel pins, angel trees, angel earrings, angel hair clips, angel hair pasta, angel art (an oxymoron?), ceramic angels, *Touched By an Angel*, Johnny Angel, Earth Angel, *Charlie's Angels*, Angel of the Morning, Anaheim Angels, Blue Angels, angelfish, angel food cake, and even the fools rushing in where angels fear to tread fill our lives with hints of haloes. Angels are hotter than . . . uh . . . they are really, really hot. Books about angels (including *The Complete Idiot's Guide to Angels*—available in paperback) describe how powerful angels make everything right (and make the authors lots of money).

Television shows portray beautiful, sensitive angels who make everything right (and get good ratings).

This newsletter column is offered with apologies to Frank Church, editor of *The New York Sun*, who wrote a vaguely similar piece in 1897.

Dear Author of *Who Moved My Pulpit? A Hilarious Look at Ministerial Life*,

I am eight years old. Some of my little friends say there are no angels. Papa says, "If you see it in a book published by Smyth & Helwys it's so." Please tell me the truth, are there angels?

Virginia O'Hanlon

Virginia,

Your little friends are wrong. They have been affected by the skepticism of a skeptical age. They do not believe in what they can't see. They think that nothing can be which is not comprehensible by their little tiny minds. All minds, Virginia, whether they be adults' or children's—even ministers'—are little. In this great universe of ours, people are mere ants in their intellects.

Yes, Virginia, there are angels. They exist as certainly as love and generosity and devotion exist, and you know that they abound and give your life beauty and joy. Alas! How dreary would be the world if there were no angels! It would be as dreary as if there were no ministers. There would be no childlike faith then, no poetry, no romance, and no Cameron Diaz kicking tail to make tolerable this existence. Not believe in angels! You might get your papa to hire photographers to try to take a picture of Drew Barrymore, but even if they could not find any angels to photograph, what would that prove? If nobody sees angels, does that mean that there are no angels? As a rule, people see only what they expect to see. Some of your little friends may point out that Nicholas Cage in *City of Angels* and all the *Angels in the Outfield* seem silly. What does that have to do with the ways in which the Spirit of God is present in magnificent, holy, unexplainable moments, in a gentle whisper, or a wisp of light? The most real things in the world are those that neither children nor adults can see. Did you ever see hope touch a broken heart? Of course not, but that's no proof that hope is not there. Nobody can conceive or imagine all the wonders there are unseen and unseeable in the world.

No angels! Thank God! They live and live forever. A thousand years from now, Virginia, nay ten times ten thousand years from now, they will continue to make our hearts glad.

Harry Potter and the Lake of Fire

One of a pastor's responsibilities is to interpret major cultural phenomena in the light of the gospel. Unfortunately, I've never seen *Joe Millionaire*, but I have read the Harry Potter books. Harry has sold a bazillion books in at least twenty-eight languages—including Icelandic and Serbo-Croatian. As those of you who read Icelandic and Serbo-Croatian know, shortly before his eleventh birthday, skinny, bespectacled orphan Harry Potter learns that he is a wizard. Harry has been raised by the interminably mean Dursleys (who give Muggles a bad name), so he is glad to board the train from platform nine and three-quarters to go to the Hogwarts School of Witchcraft and Wizardry—which is eerily similar to a seminary. The story is not, however, about potions, cauldrons, and sorcerers, so much as it is about loneliness, love, and loyalty.

That's why I was shocked when I received an urgent e-mail from praise2victoryinchrist@yahoo.com warning me about "the curse of an abomination with which Satan seeks to fill our land." I assumed it would be a prophetic word against racism, sexism, or materialism, but as I read further I was shocked to learn that parents are encouraging their children in "a demonic recruitment into Satanism and witchcraft of mass proportions" (a threat presumably greater than that posed by Barney the Dinosaur). These foolish parents are taking their children to see movies that "make demonic possession look harmless, useful, even funny."

If only praise2victoryinchrist@yahoo.com had warned us earlier. You see, and I hesitate to admit this, my family and I have seen the Harry Potter movies. We honestly didn't feel like we were participating in a "massive demonic assault against our children and families." As a rule, Carol and I steer clear of demonic assaults against our children.

In fact, and I know that I am endangering your immortal soul—it seemed like fun. But now I realize how blind I was! When we went to *Harry Potter and the Chamber of Secrets*, the movie didn't start on time, and a group of young girls started chanting "Harry Potter, Harry Potter." It seemed innocuous, but they were obviously trying to lure other second graders into their coven!

Or maybe the lesson we need to remember is that sometimes Christians are goofy. Fundamentalists, many of whom are mad about Harry, have led school districts to ban the books. The stated fear is that reading about wizards, spells, and imagination will lead children to join a cult. The Arkansas Baptist Convention passed a resolution condemning the Harry Potter books and movies. (There is still no word on how Arkansas Baptists feel about *The Wizard of Oz, Alice in Wonderland*, or *The Chronicles of Narnia*.) This is one of those occasions on which well-meaning Christians should be ignored. We hope that non-Christians don't paint us all with the same brush. Judging Christianity by praise2victoryinchrist@ yahoo.com is like judging music by Celine Dion, Mexican food by Taco Bell, or preaching by, well, use your imagination.

I never responded to praise2victoryinchrist@yahoo.com, because all I could think to write was: "Dear P2ViC, I know you're not going to like this, but I saw the movie and thought it was okay, though not as good as the book. You might want to consider lightening up. You are, of course, right that there are real enemies of God's grace out there, but Harry isn't one of them. Have you thought about going after *Veggie Tales*?"

A Cleansing Sacrament

Books on the spiritual disciplines include prayer, Scripture, worship, fasting, meditation, and so on, but because of their timidity, the authors make a glaring omission. The most neglected spiritual practice, by far, is laundry. In Exodus 19:10, "The Lord said unto Moses, Go unto the people and sanctify them today and tomorrow, and let them wash their clothes." It's no coincidence that angels are usually pictured in bright—which might be interpreted "just out of the dryer"—clothing. When John Wesley said, "Cleanliness is next to godliness," he was on to a vital truth. As with other spiritual disciplines, we are tempted to let initial failures keep us from trying again. Most of us have had bad experiences with reds and whites that became pinks. Those disappointments, which may have come while we were still immature in our faith, should not lead us to say, "I'm no spiritual giant. Laundry's not for me." We need to ask, "What are the keys to growing spiritually through laundry?"

Simplicity is crucial. Avoid products with names like the "Wonder Washing Disc." Don't give much attention to fancy fabric softeners, starch, bleach, and ironing. Use less detergent than the principalities and powers that be tell you to use. Laundry that deepens our journey is straightforward washing in the normal cycle with no frills.

Sorting is a way of appreciating the diversity within creation. Spirituality is free, but it's also ordered, so read labels. Recognize the difference between permanent press and delicate, but don't see that difference as a negative; it's a gift. Sort carefully, but every once in a while, playfully toss a pair of old white socks into a blue load just to see what happens. Wash in all temperatures, but use hot only when absolutely necessary. When you spray a tough, greasy spot with stain remover, think about the prophet Jeremiah: "For though thou wash thee with nitre, and take thee with much soap, yet thine iniquity is marked" (2:22). Be glad that you have a can of Shout instead of nitre.

Laundry and spirituality take time. Don't be in a hurry. Wisdom knows that two minutes in the spin cycle saves twenty in the dryer. Be still and listen to the washer making the world cleaner. Fold the clothes in quiet reflection. Clear your mind and try not to think too much when you're folding. I used to ask mistakenly, "Why do I wash the towels so much? Aren't we clean when we use them?" When you hang up shirts, realize that you are stating your hope in the future. Pairing socks is an act of reconciliation, but don't worry when a sock escapes from the dryer. It will find its place. Remember that it's not the clothes that make the man or woman; it's folding the clothes. Don't live every day as if it's your last—or you'll never wash clothes.

Doing someone else's laundry is an expression of agape love. Though folding is usually a time for solitude, it must be taught to and shared with children. Begin with age-appropriate folding. Don't give your five-year-old a fitted sheet; it's cruel (though undeniably amusing). Some people find meaning in praying as they fold: "Thank you for the socks that will cover my feet. Where should my feet take me tomorrow?" If you pray over your laundry, do so silently. If someone hears and expresses admiration for your spirituality, you may become proud.

In his farewell speech to the Hebrew people (Deut 29:5), Moses said, "I have led you forty years in the wilderness; your clothes are not waxen upon you." We should be grateful for our clothes that are not waxen. In Revelation 7:14, the ones who come through the tribulation "have washed their robes." The people who do laundry, who are "clothed with righteousness," live deeper, fuller lives.

In his seventeenth-century classic of Christian devotion, *The Practice of the Presence of God*, Brother Lawrence tells of discovering God while washing pots and pans: "I possess God as peacefully in the bustle of my kitchen, as I do upon my knees before the Holy Sacrament. My faith becomes enlightened. It seems to me that the curtain of obscurity is drawn, and that the endless cloudless day of the other life is dawning." We can only imagine how enlightened he would have been if, instead of the kitchen, he had been in charge of the laundry.

Every minister should speak to perplexing issues in order to keep his or her own soul alive. Just as cherubs, wizards, and washing can be joyfully addressed, ministers should use humor as they deal with issues such as capital punishment, abortion, and war—or maybe not.

eleven

And All I Got
Was This Lousy T-shirt

Methodists, Baptists, Episcopalians, and Republicans frequently get together for business, education, fellowship, and something resembling worship. At many religious meetings, the primary question is "Aren't you glad you're not at that other meeting?"

In groups of more than five pastors, someone inevitably asks, "How's your church doing?" The answer is often something like "We're okay, but we're starting the summer slump. I hope the giving doesn't fall as much as last year." A few ministers answer, "The Holy Spirit is really at work. Our church is on fire." Those ministers have trouble getting other ministers to sit with them.

Some ministers think they get together to compare their latest successes. When a misunderstanding clergy asks you, "How big is your church?" be a discerning minister and give one of these two answers:

"It's about five thousand. We have four services, but only one is televised."

OR

"It was a big church when I got there, but now I've gotten it down to a size I can handle. There are about nine left. I think I'll keep most of them."

Be sure to alternate the two answers given above—even if it's the same person asking.

Bland Tacos

The stated agenda for most religious meetings is to greet, introduce, recognize, pray, nominate, elect, report, recommend, motion, move, second, debate, amend, refer, question, resolve, adopt, approve, and defeat like nobody's business, but it's not that simple. These suggestions on how to attend a convention may seem so obvious that they should go unwritten, but they are offered in the hope that one needy minister can be helped:

Never go to a convention for which you have to pay. This is not an experience for which you should get a bill.

"Box lunch" is an oxymoron.

If you want to make a motion that will pass, move to close debate. I have been to my state convention enough to know that this motion always passes: "Mr. President, I am Reverend Joe Billy Bob, pastor of the First Baptist Church of Possum Kingdom, Texas, home of the Fighting Armadillos, Class 1A football champs, 1993. I rejoice that Texas Baptists are spreading the gospel from Amarillo to Brownsville, from El Paso to Marshall, in Houston and Cut and Shoot, in Dallas and Blanket, in San Antonio and Christmas, in Corpus Christi and Noodle, in Fort Worth and Dime Box. The gospel is being shared with old and young, rich and poor, conservative and more conservative, native Texan and foreign interloper. I move that we stop doing all this discussing and do what Baptists do best. I move we vote."

Take a book. Stop reading during prayers, but everything else is fair game.

Pay attention. This may seem contradictory to the previous tip, but there's not a lot to which you should pay attention, so you can do both. Convention planners have noticed that 95 percent of those who attend have gray hair. In response, they occasionally ask some-one "creative" to do something "creative." When the Swahili dancers begin their missions presentation, don't miss the fascinating reactions of the other gray-haired ministers.

Generally speaking, the people on the dais are not the spiciest tacos on the menu. Conventions allow people who love budgets, motions, and resolutions to hold the rest of us hostage. They get to do this because they have actually read *Robert's Rules of Order*.

Stay out of whatever room has the most ministers in it. Will Rogers said, "Methodist preachers are like manure. Spread them around, they do a lot of good. Pile 'em all together in one place, they get to stinking."

Talking in the halls is more fun than sitting in the hall. Check name tags quickly. An old classmate, your sister-in-law's cousin, and anyone who knows your organist is more interesting than whoever is behind the microphone.

Counseling Services Magic Jar Openers

While the arena is painfully dull, the exhibit area sounds, smells, and tastes are amazing. The Minnesota-Wisconsin Partnership busily cuts pieces of cheese and wraps them around apple slices to entice hungry people to talk about St. Paul or Green Bay. Get there early to pick up one of the buttons that says, "Jesus is coming to South Carolina. Get ready." Look for the publishing house that sells bundles of books in sealed brown paper wrappers labeled only "Preaching Grab Bag—$10" and "Spirituality Grab Bag—$12."

As Yogi Berra put it, "You can hear a lot by listening." You'll hear these remarks more than once:

"If you take the Tootsie Roll, you have to take the brochure."

"I'm not jaded yet, but I've only been here thirty minutes."

"I always end up sitting in front of the crying baby."

"Unfortunately, those with our polity need more sense than those who are not self-governing."

Before you leave, grab a tote bag and pick up your weight in free souvenirs: WWJD bracelets; Christian university buttons; denominational ink pens; nondenominational pencils; retirement program note pads; children's ministry balloons; church loan corporation coin purses; ministerial insurance letter openers; children's home refrigerator magnets; counseling services magic jar openers (better mental health through kitchen aids!); family services chip clips (quietly reducing family tension); and intercultural initiatives hacky sacks (hacky sacks cross cultural lines). This quasi-religious version of trick or treat is the highlight of any convention.

We're Not in Kansas Anymore

Many of the previously mentioned tips for conventions are also helpful when enduring continuing education opportunities. Young ministers attend seminars with titles like "Building Vibrant

Congregations for Tomorrow's World." Well-paid church gurus from the Church Growth Leadership/Discipleship Institute (who last served on church staffs twenty-five years ago, but are frequently quoted in *Christianity Today*) come down from the mountain to say, "Society is changing. The church must change, too. Young people don't go to church like they used to. Get some young couples with babies."

Feel good that you already know it all. Act enthralled as the spiritual guide fervently says, "Churches have to realize that they are not in Kansas anymore and prepare for an Oz where members must engage a whole new world."

The clergy, many of whom signed on hoping to be in charge, are told to train the laity, many of whom signed on hoping someone else would be in charge, to lead. Those who are failing with new models of ministry are encouraged. Those whose old models of ministry are working are chastised.

The sages tell ministers what we thought was obvious—to keep evaluating the meaningfulness of church programs. Are we being challenged and challenging others? Is our focus on mission and ministry? Are we spending church funds on trips when we could have stayed home and read *Leadership*?

The maharishis talk about "exploring changing paradigms of thought." They explain that "under Christendom" (which can be dated from the fourth century to Jimmy Swaggart's first nationally televised crying jag), "whole countries were thought to be Christian, and so missions was defined as expanding the empire." Now churches must provide donuts.

Raise your hand now and then. Experts on the church of the future need to be pressed for details. Do disposable communion sets make the Lord's Supper the Lord's Snack? Should the person who runs PowerPoint be called the minister of software? Is it wrong for Christian aerobicizers to call themselves "firm believers"?

If a continuing education event is going slowly, count how many of these phrases you hear: changing paradigms, declining congregations, mission strategies, re-visioning your call, ministerial effectiveness, transforming stewardship, creative approaches, small groups, systemic understanding, congregational megatrends, and break for lunch. This exercise helps regain your own interest.

If your church expert isn't holding anyone's attention, you can be helpful. Ask, "Are preachers getting shorter? I have no statistics on this, but my impression is that 6'4" Adonises with deep booming voices no longer go into ministry. Do short people feel a greater need to be called to something?" A simple question such as this lights up the dullest seminar. Your motivational messiah will thank you.

John Wesley said that "Christian conferencing" is a means of grace. He was right about a lot of other things.

A Complete Lack of Talent

I was at a convention eating lunch with six other pastors when one said, "We're far from home. We're all friends. What would you be if you could be something else?"

We looked around to see if we were among friends. A weary colleague began, "When I was in college I wanted to be an architect, but I didn't think that I could do the math. Some days I think that I was smart enough after all."

A second minister said, "My favorite part of being a pastor is visiting sick people. Every time I walk into a hospital I wish I was a doctor."

Another offered, "When I read a book by Philip Yancey, I think 'That's the life.' The only thing that keeps me from being a writer is a complete lack of talent."

Someone wistfully said, "I dream of being a pastor, but I always dream of being the pastor of some other church."

"I just want to be a rich church member who calls the pastor on Monday to complain."

Even with the joy of conventions and continuing education, every now and then we all wish for something else.

Foghorn Leghorn

When ministers want to be Frank Lloyd Wright, they need not panic. People in every profession think about the roads not taken. The ministry is difficult, dangerous, wearying, and wonderful. Left unchecked, the busyness of a minister's life makes us identify with Abraham Maslow: "The only tool in your closet is a hammer and everything in the world looks strangely like a nail." We need to balance tension-filled days with play. Ministers should be more serious in their pursuit of fun.

Golf works for some ministers. I've never played a round of golf that didn't involve a windmill, but after winning a round of golf on the radio, I called a church member who knows the game. He suggested that I hit a bucket of balls at a driving range before actually playing the round to increase my enjoyment. It seemed easy enough—baseball with a stationary target. As I prepared to smack my first fearsome drive, he explained, "Your right hand should be over your left, feet shoulder-width apart, and knees slightly bent. Bring the club back with your left arm straight and right elbow bent (which seems to indicate that the best golfer would be someone whose left arm is six inches shorter than the right), wrist cocked, chin down, eyes on the ball, and feet straight ahead. Swing naturally." The only thing less natural than swinging a golf club is actually hitting a golf ball, which I did only by chance. I spent thirty minutes digging up six square yards of turf and perfecting a slice that can, with a good bounce, travel as far as fifty yards. My friend tried to be encouraging: "That was a good swing. It would have been great if you had hit it." I have given up any subconscious dream of being Tiger Woods and understand why Mark Twain said, "Golf is a good walk spoiled." I thought I would do better with a tennis racket.

So I called a church member who plays tennis. I haven't played tennis since 1982 when I finished my college phys-ed requirement. (My grandparents were sure our educational system was bankrupt if you could get college credit for tennis.) I used what I had learned playing golf—"left arm straight, right elbow bent, wrist cocked, swing naturally"—but still ended up with a slice that travels, without a bounce, as far as fifty yards. My tennis friend tried to be encouraging: "That was a good swing. It would have been great if you had hit it." We came up with rules to make us more evenly matched: I could hit the ball in the doubles court; I could let the ball bounce more than once on my side; no backhands; my opponent had to play left-handed, use a ping-pong paddle, or wear a blindfold. I have given up any subconscious dream of being Andre Agassi and understand why Mark Twain played more golf than tennis.

I have tried less athletic recreation. One young adult Sunday school class gathers on Friday nights—primarily because someone else cares for their children—to play "Chicken Foot," an infrequently delightful domino game. Chicken Foot combines the frustration of Parcheesi with the intricate strategy of Chutes and Ladders. In the spirit of Chicken Foot players take nicknames related to chicken—"Grandy's," "Chow Mein," "Kentucky Fried," "Ducky Lucky," "Cocky Locky," "Goosey Lucy" and "Quick Draw" (that one's not chicken-related, but was descriptive of the strategy of going to the bone yard early and often); I fulfilled a subconscious dream of being "Foghorn Leghorn." Keeping my left arm straight and right elbow bent didn't help. Carol tries to be encouraging: "That was a good move. It would be great if it was legal." I can't imagine Mark Twain playing Chicken Foot, but if he was a minister he might.

Can I Buy a Vowel?

Networking, continuing education, and exercise are all essential for ministers, but our calling still requires serious soul-searching. During those times, think about Vanna White.

Do you remember when Vanna switched from turning the letters to touching a switch? The headline in our local paper was an attention grabber—"Vanna will be pushing some buttons." The story out of Culver City, California, explained that "Vanna White's job as the renowned letter-turner on TV's *Wheel of Fortune* just got a little easier." Producer Harry Friedman (who should have been commended for his willingness to make what I thought would be a controversial decision) said, "It's true that Vanna will no longer turn letters. Instead, she will turn them on." The new puzzle board allowed White to touch a switch to display correct letters picked by contestants.

The pastoral counselor in me wondered whether this was a sign that years of letter-turning aged Vanna before her time. At one point, the then forty-year-old White says, "The new puzzle board was designed especially for me." Concerned viewers watched carefully to see if Vanna was physically less capable of turning letters that twisted so effortlessly ten years ago.

Cynics wondered about the statement that Vanna's job "just got a little easier" and asked, "How could Vanna's job get any easier?"

Intelligent people asked, "Is *Wheel of Fortune* still on?" Even more intelligent people asked, "What's *Wheel of Fortune*?"

For me the most striking quote (among many) was from the ebullient letter-turner turned button-pusher, Vanna herself, "I've always felt that I have the most fun job on television. Now, it's going to be even better." Like other contemplative ministers, I immediately began comparing my job with hers. Would I trade jobs with Vanna White?

When I am in a ministerial quandary, I often ponder the hidden truths to be found in *Wheel of Fortune* (which is, after all, a game based on hidden truths). A minister's job and Vanna's job are quite similar. We both get to dress up in glamorous outfits. She works with words; ministers work with words. Most of our problems seem hard at first, but things usually work out eventually. We both work with nice people. (Wouldn't Pat Sajak make a great deacon?)

This is not meant to minimize the differences between our professions. Vanna wears each outfit once; ministers often wear the same outfit each Sunday. Unlike the contestants on the show, preachers are not paid by the word—though some preach as if they are. On *Wheel of Fortune*, there is only one big winner. In the church, everyone gets all the grace there is.

One of the biggest differences is that turning on letters seems (and I mean no disrespect) somewhat limiting. Most jobs, even ones as fascinating as Vanna's, tend to narrow one's perspective. Some jobs make the lives of those who fill them seem smaller until they start believing that touching a switch rather than turning a letter is a major life change. Solving the puzzles becomes more important than asking the big questions.

Ministers are fortunate to deal with big questions. When I was at seminary I had friends who had given up on the institutional church. They were willing to consider any religious job that wasn't church-related because they were afraid of the constraints of pastoral ministry. None of them stuck around long enough to know the joy of serving with a genuine church.

The best congregations, far from constraining any thinking their ministers might do, act as catalysts to help us think in broader terms. If we're fortunate, and paying attention, we will see that we are surrounded by people who ask the big questions: How does Christianity relate to other world religions? What does it mean to be as truly inclusive as Jesus was? How can a church go beyond what is expected? How do we avoid getting caught up in trivialities? How should we spend our lives?

A crucial question for most people is, "Does my job lead me to hear only small questions or deal with the big picture?" By that criteria, ministers have a wonderful job. Vanna should be so lucky.

(conclusion)

Audacious Underwear

A few years ago, H. Jackson Brown's *Life's Little Instruction Book* spent several months on the best-sellers' lists. The book is 511 suggestions, observations, and reminders about how to live a happy and rewarding life. It offers a plethora of helpful advice. Buy whatever kids are selling on card tables in their front yards. Put marshmallows in your hot chocolate. Wear audacious underwear under the most solemn business attire. Turn off the television at dinnertime. Let your children overhear you saying complimentary things. Sit down front at meetings. Have a friend who owns a truck. Be good to your minister. (It's not in the book, but it should be.)

Life's Little Instruction Book for Ministers is waiting to be written. Wear comfortable shoes to the church office, then take them off. Compliment choir members. Get a bumper sticker that says in big letters "Jesus"; in medium type, "Save me"; in tiny letters, "from your followers." Put it on your car, but only for a week. Learn the name of a child each Sunday. Pray during the prelude. Gravitate toward kind people. Don't spend much time around those who make it hard to breathe. Call several members of a Sunday school class who were absent and congratulate them on being elected class president. Don't ever mail it in. When a church member says,

"I was going to throw out these ties, but then I thought you might wear them," respond, "I need a pay raise, don't I?" Hug deacons. Play a deep right field for the church softball team. Tell the person seated next to you in worship to sing louder. Tell a worship leader that you thought her prayer was wonderful, but wondered if the obscenity was a slip of the tongue. Pretend you are a greeter. Ask visitors if they prefer smoking or nonsmoking. Keep the nice notes. Throw the others away. Pray for people you don't love. Put up a sign in the foyer—"Sweet Potato Queens Meeting after worship in the parlor"—just to see who shows up. Imagine Gloria Swanson saying, "I'm still big, it's the churches that got small." Take every opportunity to fall in love with your church. Keep books that raise eyebrows on your desk—Bishop John Shelby Spong, Pat Robertson. Take your vacation days.

Without Church

Ministers need to keep in mind how much we would miss without the church. Without church most men would never sing in public sober. Organ companies would be out of business. Weddings would be shorter. We'd have to buy our own coffee on Sundays. The phrase "food, fun, and fellowship" would never have been coined. Fewer people would experience the joy of being on a committee. No books would have zippered covers. Rosaries would just be beads. Fewer women would be named Mary and men Joseph. Every softball league would center on beer.

Christmas tree farms would be real farms. Manheim Steamroller would play Arbor Day tunes. The Mitford series would be about a genial small-town elementary school principal. The New Orleans Saints would have a more fitting nickname. Fanny Crosby would have written Hallmark cards. Rick Warren would have no purpose. Anne Lamott would write depressing books. Jabez wouldn't have a prayer.

There would be nothing to "come, come, come, come, come" to in the "wildwood" or the "dale." The five points of Calvinism would be reduced to zero. George Burns would star in movies called *Oh*. Dana Carvey would just be "the Lady." The Beatitudes would be the name of a rock band.

There'd be less children's art on refrigerators. Funerals wouldn't be nearly so uplifting. Youth ministers would be cruise directors. Church secretaries would have high-paying jobs. Pastors would be working the drive-through.

Remember

Though ministry can be hectic, pastors get paid for doing what they love. Remember how fortunate you are. Remember the first time you came to your church and what it felt like to walk into the sanctuary. Remember the people who invited you. Remember the grace that got you to your church. Remember your first baptism and how sacred it felt. Remember the first time someone at your church hugged you and how good it felt. Remember when you learned which church member knows more Bible verses than you do.

Remember the best play the church ever did, and the worst. Remember Vacation Bible School—how much fun it is when it starts and how wonderful if feels when it's over. Remember youth camp, picnics, and mission trips. Remember Advent and Christmas Eve. Remember Maundy Thursday, Good Friday, and Easter.

Remember how holy it felt to know that people were praying for you when you were sick. Remember the people who came and went, but made you love them while they were there. Remember the funerals, the people who ought to still be around. Remember a moment in worship when the grace of God was so good it had to be true. Remember it all, because when you remember Christ's church, you'll be grateful again.

Give Thanks

Be thankful for the people who were preparing your church long before you got there and for everyone who makes your church a home. Be thankful that you belong to a church that opens it doors to someone like you. Be thankful for the ministry your church does. There are people better cared for because you're there.

Be thankful if you belong to a church where the staff loves the congregation (it's less common than most think). Be thankful that in your church people have met the best friends they will ever have; that someone who felt completely alone got a phone call at just the right time; that people devastated by the death of someone they loved let your congregation slowly show them life again.

Be thankful for the good times: the precious people who love you more than you deserve; the ones who make you a better minister just by being there; the times that you're better than you know how to be. Be thankful for the joy in your congregation.

Remember and be thankful, for in memory and gratitude we discover that God has been here all along leading us to joy. The best thing your ministry has going for it, the thing for which you should give the most thanks, the thing you most need to remember, is the presence of God. Ministers are never alone. A grace bigger than you pulls you along and makes your ministry unique.

A Sacred Benediction

When I came to my present church, I was in charge of a staff meeting for the first time. At our initial gathering I asked for help in composing a pastoral benediction to close each meeting. We talked about the benedictions you would expect ("The Lord bless you and keep you"), but as we thought about who ministers need to be to serve the church, we ended up with "Let's have some fun out there."

This benediction has served us well. When we go through tragedies, it's "Even in the midst of overwhelming sadness, on the night before he died Jesus said, 'I have said these things that my joy might be in you.' Let's have some fun out there."

When we're in the middle of a busy week, it's "Even in the midst of a crowded schedule, remember that Jesus said, 'I have come that you might have life abundantly.' Let's have some fun out there."

I've offered this benediction more than one hundred times. God calls us in these holy, sacred words to deeper ministry: "Let's have some fun out there."

Study Questions for Small Groups

(preface)
What did you think of *Footloose*?

(introduction)
How would you tell the story of the Ethiopian Eunuch to four-year-olds?

(one) Calling
What is the best topping for enchiladas?

(two) Your First Church
On whom would you like to see a criminal background check?

(three) Preaching
What should happen to people who sleep during sermons?

(four) Worship
Do you need a haircut?

(five) Administration

Would you rather be a church secretary?

(six) Evangelism, Education, Ministry, and Pastoral Care

Would you like to have a sign that says "The Best Vitamin for Christians—B1" in front of your church?

(seven) Children, Youth, and Senior Adults

Children's camp, youth camp, or a month playing dominos? Discuss.

(eight) Christian Year

Christmas, Easter, baseball, or football? Discuss.

(nine) Church Newsletters

What do you think happened to the author after his April 1st newsletter? What should have happened?

(ten) Theology

Which one of Charlie's Angels is your favorite?

(eleven) Continuing Education

Would Vanna White be a good Sunday school teacher?

(conclusion)

Are you having any fun?

(bibliography)

Anderson, Bernhard W. *Understanding the Old Testament*. Englewood Cliffs NJ: Prentice-Hall, 1982.

Blanchard, Kenneth H., and Paul Hersey. *Management of Organizational Behavior: Utilizing Human Resources*. Englewood Cliffs NJ: Prentice-Hall, 1982.

Blech, Benjamin, and Jay Stevenson. *The Complete Idiot's Guide to Angels*. New York: Alpha Books, 1999.

Footloose. Directed by Herbert Ross. 1984.

Krantz, Les. *Jobs Rated Almanac: The Best and Worst Jobs*. Hoboken NJ: John Wiley & Sons, Inc., 2002.

Ridenhour, Fritz. *How to Be a Christian Without Being Religious*. Glendale CA: G/L Publications, 1974.

Robert, Henry M. *The Scott-Foresman Robert's Rules of Order*. New York: HarperCollins, 1991.

Rowling, J. K. *Harry Potter and the Order of the Phoenix*. New York: Scholastic, 2003.

Schweizer, Eduard. *Ego Eimi . . . Die Religionsgeschichtliche Herkunft und theologische Bedeuting der Johannesischen Bildreden, zugleich ein Beitrag zur Quellenfrage des vierten Evangeliums*. Gottingen: Vandenhoeck & Ruprecht, 1939.

Segal, Erich. *Love Story*. New York: Harper & Row, 1970.

Shakespeare, William. *The Tragedy of King Lear*. Ed. Russell Fraser. New York: Signet, 1998.

Sing 'n' Celebrate II. Comp. Robert C. Black et al. Waco TX: Word Inc, 1975.

Smith, Charles M. *How to Become a Bishop Without Being Religious*. New York: Doubleday, 1965.

The Ten Commandments. Directed by Cecil B. DeMille. 1956.

Wells, Alexander T. *Commercial Aviation Safety*. New York: McGraw-Hill Professional, 2001.

Whisenant, Edgar C. *88 Reasons Why the Rapture Could Be in 1988*. Nashville: World Bible Society, 1988.